Classic English
Interiors

Classic English Interiors

Henrietta Spencer-Churchill

Photography by Andreas von Einsiedel

Little, Brown and Company (Canada) Limited

Boston • New York • London • Toronto

First published in Great Britain in 1990 by
Anaya Publishers Ltd

This Canadian edition published by
Little, Brown Canada
148 Yorkville Avenue
Toronto, Ontario
M5R 1C2

1 3 5 7 9 8 6 4 2

Canadian Cataloguing in Publication Data

Spencer-Churchill, Henrietta, 1958-
Classic English Interiors

1st Canadian ed.
ISBN 0-316-14280-8

1. Interior decoration – England.   2. Manors – England.
3. Blenheim Palace (England).   I. Einsiedel, Andreas.
II. Titre.

NK.2044.A1S64 1997   728.8 0942   C97-930597-7

Editor Alexandra Parsons
Design The Magill Design Company
Art Director Cherriwyn Magill
Designer Elaine Hewson
Photographer Andreas von Einsiedel
Stylist Jacky Boase

Project Co-ordinator Marie-Louise Leschallas

Typeset in Great Britain by Tradespools, Frome, Somerset
Printed in Hong Kong

I would firstly like to thank Maggie Pearlstine who initiated this book and who has been a great support since. Secondly I would like to thank Yvonne McFarlane at Anaya and the professional team she put together to work on the book, notably my editor Alexandra Parsons, the art director Cherriwyn Magill, the excellent photographer Andreas von Einsiedel, his assistant Richard Allenby-Pratt and Jacky Boase, the stylist.

I would also like to thank all those who work for me, my partner Zoë in particular and my assistant Marie Louise Leschallas for her endless patience in organizing the photography and typing my illegible text. My thanks also go to Ian Walton for his help in writing the text on many of the jobs he has supervised.

Thanks, too, to all my family for their cooperation in allowing their homes to be photographed and to all those friends and clients both mentioned and not for kindly allowing us to photograph their homes.

I would also like to thank Richard for giving me endless encouragement at my weekends of writing and my two wonderful sons, David and Maximilian for their enthusiasm and longing for the book to be in a shop window!

Lastly, but not least, I would like to thank Tim Chadwick for his expert advice on publishing and on how to handle publishers!

CONTENTS

PART TWO

THE LEXICON 144

INTRODUCTION

In putting this book together I have tried to give an overall impression of Classic English style which is, after all, the style I grew up with and the style most associated with my work. It is a style that exudes a warm welcome and promises comfort along with elegance and practicality. It is also versatile. In my capacity as an interior decorator, I have been asked to work on many kinds of projects, from grand country houses to budget schemes for tiny apartments, corporate schemes for hotels, revamps of single rooms, and even a motor cruiser.

In the second part of the book, The Lexicon, I have pinpointed the various elements that contribute to making the whole. Attention to detail is important throughout the decorating process, from first decisions about paint finishes and choice of fabric trimming to finishing touches like flowers and plants.

Taste and style are very personal and individual matters. As an interior designer I do not like to impose my taste onto a client, or insist that my ideas are the only ones that will work. The skills of an interior designer lie in interpreting the clients' wishes, observing their lifestyle and coaxing out of them what they really want, which is often to be read between the lines. The next challenge is to put together a solid brief and produce a professional job that the client is happy to live with.

I always consider each new project, however large or small, as having unique possibilities – rather like every new hand in a bridge game. One is presented with various elements and the satisfaction in the game – and the design project – lies in interpreting these elements to the best possible effect.

I hope that in this book you will find ideas and inspirations that may apply to your home and your lifestyle and that you will enjoy the satisfaction of getting the best out of the unique possibilities that your home presents.

Henrietta Spencer-Churchill

PART ONE

THE LOOK

THE ORIGINS OF CLASSIC ENGLISH STYLE

Defining Classic English style is not an easy task. As with all things traditionally English, words like 'good quality', 'understated' and 'timeless' spring to mind. But this has not always been the case. There was a time when there was no English style as such. What was fashionable in one European court soon became fashionable in another. Craftsmen copied each other's designs from the pattern books and basically what was available was what was available.

The English fashion for tasteful restraint set in during the first half of the 18th century, when the grand homes of Europe were typically awash with gilded wood and rococo swirls. But in England, inspired by the work of the Italian architect Andrea Palladio and his English counterpart, Inigo Jones, simple elegance was the rage. Dado rails, friezes and cornices appeared, echoing the classic proportions of the Greek column. Symmetry and balance were to be seen everywhere, as were clear, solid colours, panelling picked out with mouldings and elegantly tailored drapery.

A country house dining room with a distinct Georgian feeling: beautiful proportions and clear, strong colours.

12

The 18th century was also the English cabinetmaker's finest hour. Chippendale, Hepplewhite and Sheraton were not only producing outstanding neo-classical pieces themselves, but their books of designs were a great influence on furniture makers as far afield as America.

Very soon, the English style was something you could recognize and label and then, of course, it started to change. Even the most fashionable interiors became more comfortable and lived-in. Chairs, instead of being arranged strictly round the walls, were grouped together for conversation and the warmth of the fire. English interior design was heading towards the overstuffed and cluttered look that we now think of as Victorian.

GROWTH AND CHANGE

But homes don't change that quickly, especially homes on the scale of the English country house, which traditionally pass from generation to generation. Such houses grow to accommodate the tastes and possessions of the new incumbent while retaining the family ties and traditions of the past. It is this organic growth, overlaid upon a classical base, that makes the English country house so distinctive and yet so infinitely variable, so gracious and yet so comfortable.

An English country house drawing room should look warm and welcoming, the seats should be generous and comfortable, the windows tall and graceful, the colour scheme a subtle blend of rich and faded colours. This lovely room has all the right attributes. During the day the room is flooded with natural light, at night the strategically placed lamps create intimate pools of illumination.

BACKGROUND AND INFLUENCES

Most of my childhood was spent in the country in and around Oxfordshire. As is the case with most children, my vision was limited to my own domain – as far as I was concerned, Oxfordshire was the heart of England, a beautiful county with a large proportion of classic houses set in landscaped parks or manicured gardens. I was fortunate enough to live in one of the most beautiful Georgian houses in Oxfordshire, as well as having access to many others because they were home to relations of my father or mother.

I was also extremely lucky to be surrounded by a very large family, many of whom had considerable artistic flair in one form or another. My maternal grandmother was a talented watercolourist of landscapes and floral scenes. She and my grandfather were also superb gardeners and together created the gardens of Pusey House which they subsequently opened to the public. Her sister, my great-aunt Countess Peggy Munster, lived in a manor house at Bampton where she cultivated an English garden. She also had exquisite taste and the

Big, bold rooms can take bold colours. This wonderful
red is complemented by painted stonework.

house was decorated in an informal, elegant style. My mother is also a talented artist although she does not use her talent to paint or draw. She has always had an incredible eye for detail and an enormous flair for decorating and creating the comfortable and relaxed atmosphere that every home should have.

On my father's side there is a considerable legacy too. My grandfather was a gifted Sunday painter who enjoyed gardening to such an extent that he created his own private garden at Blenheim. There were others on that side of the family of course, including Winston Churchill and Susan Blandford, the 5th Duchess of Marlborough, who painted exquisite floral watercolours on which I have based my 'Blenheim Collection' fabrics.

Although unaware as to how my life was to develop, I can remember as a child always being very inquisitive about other people's houses. Whenever I went somewhere new with one of my parents or to a friend's house, I would love to be shown around the house, or to explore by myself.

Obviously I do not recall all the details of these explorations, but I can remember enjoying comparing the houses I had seen with the ones I lived in, and analyzing why I liked certain rooms better than others. I enjoyed looking at the way other people lived, the colours they used, their paintings, furniture and collections and from observing these I would mentally plan the way I wanted my own home to look. As time went on I would discuss other people's houses with my mother and we would talk about the things we liked or disliked and what we would change and how and why.

This natural curiosity about how people live has stood me in good stead as an interior designer, where a vital part of my work is being able to interpret what people want and subsequently provide them with a scheme suited to their lifestyle. And my experience of lifestyles does go well beyond stately homes to the cottages, houses, flats and studios belonging to people from all walks of life whom I meet during my travels.

Much of my time as a child was spent outside, riding, playing sports or helping in the garden, so the landscape and garden were another important influence. In the houses I frequented, inside and outside always seemed to be linked together and I felt quite relaxed to-ing and fro-ing from one to the other. Spending so much time in the open, I developed an enormous appreciation of light and this, too, is reflected in my work.

These, then, are the houses of my childhood, the surroundings that influenced me and played a part in forming my personal style.

The outer hall at Lee Place is a square room with a flagstone floor. The door on the right is a cupboard door, the door on the left leads to the gents' cloakroom. Walls and woodwork have been painted in a dragged, two-tone finish, the walls and the door panels being lighter than the door frames and skirtings. Natural light floods in from windows by the entrance door.

LEE PLACE

I grew up and spent the majority of my childhood in this beautiful Georgian country house. It was originally a 17th-century manor house and built as the dower house for Ditchley Park, near Charlbury. In the 1720's it was remodelled and refronted, adding the centre pediment, the four pilasters and the two single storey wings with polygonal ends. The effect was stunning, turning a perfectly normal manor house into a grand Georgian home. The back of the house is irregular and gabled and externally gives quite a different impression from the imposing front facade. The remodelling was carried out by the architect and builder Francis Smith who came from Warwick and was responsible for much work in the area.

The house is approached down a gravel driveway flanked by an avenue of lime trees. At the foot of the drive is a pair of tiny gatehouses lived in as one by the gardener. The facade of the house can be viewed across the field where cattle or horses graze. The main entrance into the house is on the opposite side and you enter

LEFT *Old stone urn on the south terrace is made from the same stone as the house. It sits in front of a huge old yew tree and on either side are traditional rose beds. The fuschia in the foreground is planted in one of the terrace's many tubs.*

RIGHT *The garden hall is the comfortable everyday room that is used for watching television, reading and relaxing. For the past 30 years the room has been decorated around the handpainted Chinese wallpaper. The green linen curtains and the matching upholstery on the sofa are the latest additions to this light and sunny room. Originally it was the main hall of the house and so it has a flagstone floor and a stone fireplace. The door on the left leads to the dining room. The French door leads to the garden.*

through a stone porch into an outer hall which has the original flagstones with inset squares of black slate. The walls and woodwork are dragged into two tones of subtle greyish/green which blend in with the marble-topped consoles. To the left of the outer hall is the gents' cloakroom which still has the original old fashioned loos with large wooden seats.

To the right of the outer hall is the inner hall which is a square, well-proportioned room off which leads the Duchess's sitting room and the central staircase. This hall is painted in the same green and has a wooden plank floor largely covered by a needlepoint rug. Although not used as a room it has a fireplace, never used now, a drum table in the centre, a long settee used for hats, gloves and newspapers and various other pieces essential to the hall of a country house, such as the barometer.

Leading from the hall towards the main staircase is the everyday sitting room called the garden hall. It was originally the main entrance hall before the Georgian additions were made. The fireplace is stone and early 18th century with a pediment on brackets and a frieze of fox masks and hunting horns. The ceiling is early 18th century and the plasterwork is original.

The Duchess's sitting room is a lovely, sunny room that overlooks the terrace. The yellow, beige and coral colour scheme is based around the Colefax & Fowler chintz used for the pinch-pleated curtains and the cushion covers. The yellow stripe wallpaper by Cole & Son enhances the warm feeling of the room. The drawing of Consuelo, the 9th Duchess, is by Helleu and the floral watercolour below is by my stepmother's mother.

OVERLEAF *The drawing room is used only for entertaining. The walls are covered in an embossed velvet, stretch battened onto the walls and trimmed with gilt wood mouldings. The arched window has a pelmet which follows the elegant shape of the curve, and the curtains, which are velvet, are trimmed with wool fringing. On the original wood plank floor is an antique rug defining the main seating area in front of the fire. The theme of golds and greens is incredibly rich and elegant. The room looks at its best in the evenings when it is filled with people and flowers and the sparkle of the chandelier.*

The walls give the impression of a hand-painted mural depicting oriental landscapes, but it is in fact a wallpaper that has not been changed for 30 years and the rest of the room has always been decorated around the walls. The curtains, recently replaced, are in a self-patterned green linen with a cream border down the lead edges and along the base. The loose covers on the armchairs are in a Colefax & Fowler chintz. The floor has the original flagstones as in the outer entrance hall and is covered by a well-worn yellow rug. It is very much a family room, housing the television and video as well as my father's desk. It has a French door leading out to the terrace on the west front of the house, hence the name, garden hall.

The door to the left of the fireplace leads to the dining room which is a large room occupying the whole of the north side of the added wings. The ceiling dates from about 1740 and is a magnificent example of rococo plasterwork. There are six wonderfully-proportioned high windows which have deep maroon red velvet curtains and the walls above the dado are painted in a lighter tone of the red verging towards a pink. The rest of the woodwork is painted in shades of grey.

To the opposite side of the garden hall is a small sitting room where the Duchess has her desk. It can also be entered from the inner hall. The curtains (which hang on spear-shaped brass poles) are a Colefax & Fowler chintz and on the walls above the dado, papered by the Duchess herself, is a Cole & Son wallpaper. Below the dado the walls are painted beige and the detail of the dado is also picked out in the same beige. The rug placed on top of the plain beige Wilton carpet is needlepoint and ties in well with the chintz.

The drawing room is in the south wing and is exactly the same shape as the dining room, though reversed. The doors are in polished hardwood and the doorcases with pediments above on brackets and carved friezes are in the style of William Kent, the 18th-century architect who designed the Royal Horse Guards Building in Whitehall. The fireplace has a frieze with a mask and leaf scrolls with an overmantel housing an oil landscape depicting the park at Blenheim before the lake was made.

The ceiling is plain with a deep enriched Georgian cornice picked out in gold leaf. The walls above the dado are fabric covered in an embossed velvet and framed with gold leaf strips. The curtains are in an ottoman fabric. The imposing pelmets with their deep swags and long tails are in the same fabric as the walls and trimmed with a white and yellow fringe. The carpet, which provides the main source of colour in the room, lies on a polished wood strip floor.

This room was decorated in about 1961 by John Fowler and the effect created is one of supreme elegance suitable for both day and night formal entertaining. The colour used on the walls and curtains is a very subtle donkey brown/grey which may appear dowdy in isolation, but it is an excellent background colour and shows off the fine furniture and paintings without distractions. The room is only used for entertaining and, when filled with fresh flowers and people, it comes alive in exactly the way it was intended to do.

The original upstairs consists of the master bedroom, dressing room and bathroom suite located on the west front, two main guest bedrooms and bathroom suites, one with a dressing room, and a further four bedrooms. Whereas the ground floor rooms are grand with good traditional proportions the upstairs is full of character on many levels. You are permanently going up or down two or three stairs leading to an adjacent room or landing and the windows are of varying styles and heights.

Above the main first floor there is an attic floor consisting of four or five rooms and cupboards located in every available space. This floor has always been used for living-in employees or for long-term storage.

In 1961–1962 my previous stepmother, Tina Livanos, built on an additional wing to the east side of the house to provide extra bedrooms for her children and a large playroom which was originally used as a cinema room. It provided an extra three bedrooms then used by her daughter Christina (Onassis) and son Alexander and later by my brother and myself.

The garden is not at all formal and consists mainly of large, well-manicured lawns with a few herbacious borders and on the west front, roses. The walled kitchen garden was always my favourite area. It is sheltered, sunny and well-tended and it produces every vegetable and fruit that it is possible to grow in England's uncertain climate.

My most favourite building is the stable block which was built in 1725 with a central wooden clock turret and a hexagonal cupola from which protrude pedimented wings. They were rarely used as working stables as the hunters were always kept at Blenheim and my pony was stabled in a separate loose box, but converted they would make a wonderful house – a project I would love to undertake and one I worked on when studying at the Inchbald School of Design.

LEFT *The front of Church House faces east and gets the morning sun. It is a red brick early Georgian house with later additions on the sides. Flower borders flank the stone porch and the stone steps that lead to the main entrance.*

RIGHT *The drawing room benefits from sun all day. The area beyond the archway is an addition to the original room, which is now a U-shape with four seating areas. One is based around the fireplace, one at the garden end and two others through the arch. The scheme is basically pink and green. It is a big room that is made more interesting with a mixture of patterns, stripes and plains.*

CHURCH HOUSE

Church House is an early Georgian red brick house in Oxfordshire at the foot of the Berkshire Downs. When my mother moved into the house in 1961 it was about half the size it is now and consisted of six bedrooms, a sitting room, a dining room and drawing room. Now, nearly 30 years later with additions and alterations made over the years, it is a spacious ten-bedroom house with a large drawing room, three sitting rooms, a dining room and kitchen.

The garden, which is about two acres, has matured along with the house and being on green sand soil, plants establish themselves easily and grow quickly. Like my grandparents, my mother is a keen gardener and having grown up at Pusey with a spectacular garden she had good grounding when it came to creating her own garden.

The house has the advantage of being very light with strategic rooms placed on both sides of the house so it is always possible to sit in a room with the sun streaming in through the window. The

Another view of the drawing room, looking east. The curtains on the bow window are dress curtains. Behind them are short curtains that draw into the window, otherwise the window seat would be out of commission in the evenings. An upholstered stool doubles as a coffee table and a club fender provides additional seating. It is a very cosy, homely room, crammed with photos and memorabilia.

rooms, although not large, are well proportioned and each has been well thought out and decorated to fulfil its particular function. My mother has a great eye for detail and every object, picture and flower arrangement is carefully selected and placed.

The drawing room, running the width of the house, has windows facing west and east. It was originally an oblong room without the addition it now has. The addition, which now makes the room almost a 'U' shape, was added about 20 years ago, incorporating an existing room which used to be an external laundry room. The room now has four separate seating areas, two fireplaces and many different focal points.

There is a round card table covered with a cloth with a banquette seat and two side chairs – this is where many a bridge game has been played or a puzzle pieced together. The area around the corner is generally used by guests wanting to read quietly or write using the mahogany bureau.

The main part of the room has, in effect, two seating groups, one around the fireplace and the other in front of the large window, which easily become one, should the need arise.

The room was totally redecorated about a year and a half ago.

My mother's study, which used to be the dining room, overlooks the terrace across to the garden and gets sun in the afternoons. It is a very pretty, light room decorated around the pink and green curtain fabric. The soft rag effect on the walls is in fact a wallpaper and, as there was no cornice in the room, my mother stencilled a border to mark the division between wall and ceiling. A three-seat sofa takes up most of the room and as there was not enough room for side tables and table lamps, we installed wall lights instead. The picture on the right is by McEwan, a painter who specializes in tulips.

The colours are now predominantly pinks and greens, chosen to compliment the Jean Munro *Polyanthus* chintz. The curtains are in a Colefax & Fowler pink stripe fabric. A shallow pelmet finishes off the curtains elegantly without cutting out the light or overwhelming the furnishings. The carpet is beige with a small cream trellis and the walls are stippled in a very pale apple green. The area around the corner has fabric battened onto the walls which gives a warmer feel and separates it from the rest of the room.

There is no overhead lighting and all the lighting is decorative. The room is atmospherically lit with table lamps, picture lights and lights within the built-in bookcases. The pictures are a mixture of oils, watercolours and prints collected over a long period.

My mother's study, which runs off the hall and faces west, was formerly the dining room and housed a round table. It is very much a passage room and therefore the furniture had to be placed leaving a walkway to one side. The curtains are an old Warners chintz and are hung on a corded pole. The walls are a simulated paint finish that is, in fact, a wallpaper. On the walls are hung a mixture of prints and plates. The desk is painted to simulate bamboo and the coffee table is brass and glass.

ABOVE *A stone urn marks a gap in a wall that leads to another part of the garden. The wall used to be a solid continuous one that blocked further vistas of the garden from the house, so the gap was made to give more depth to the view.*

ABOVE RIGHT *A 19th-century painted metalwork seat encircles only half of the tree and so it can easily be moved out of the way when the lawn has to be mown or the tree needs attention.*

RIGHT *A statue leads the eye down an avenue of intertwined trees. The dark bush behind the statue gives the vista a certain impact. The kitchen garden lies beyond, divided from other parts of the garden by planted borders.*

OVERLEAF LEFT *The main bedroom is over the drawing room and has a little balcony leading off it. The room has quite a low, sloping ceiling but it is very light and bright. The main colour in this room is a soft grey/blue, given added warmth with touches of pink. The walls have been finished off with braid as there is no cornice, and my mother has decorated the cupboard doors and the lampshades with stencils. The long shelf behind the little sofa is, in fact, a radiator cover.*

OVERLEAF RIGHT *The swimming pool pavilion is a very simple wooden structure with a trellis on the front. Stone pineapples either side give it a bit of embellishment. Inside there is a kitchenette, a changing room and a loo. It was built about 20 years ago and painted pink to match the garden side of the house.*

The master bedroom, dressing room and bathroom suite all sit over the drawing room and the bedroom and bathroom were an addition to the house when the drawing room was extended. The bedroom faces west and has a small terrace off it also looking west over the garden and onto a patio below.

The colour scheme of the bedroom and bathroom is predominantly blue and white. The walls have a blue wallpaper giving the appearance of fine linen and my mother has stencilled motifs onto the cupboard doors. She also stencilled the lampshades. The portraits over the radiator are, on the left my brother James, on the right, myself and in the centre my half-sister Larissa. The beautiful pink roses, typical of an English country garden, come from the borders overlooked from the bedroom.

There are two main double guest bedrooms with en-suite bathrooms. The one featured here was formerly the master bedroom and was decorated with a stunning old George Spencer chintz. The fabrics now used are primarily by Colefax & Fowler in reds, pinks and greens. The curtains of the corona over the bed are in a printed voile which gives an airier feel than having the whole corona in the chintz. There is also a matching blanket cover in the

Two views of the main guest bedroom, which used to be the main bedroom until the new wing was built. The scheme is a successful mix of pattern and stripe. The room was designed around the curtain chintz, using the existing furniture. Part of the wallpaper stripe was cut off and used horizontally to finish off the top of the wall and it looks very effective. The chintz was used sparingly on the bed, the curtains of the corona are in a lovely printed voile which gives a light and airy feel to the room. The bamboo tables either side of the sofa were picked up in a junk shop.

voile under the bedspread. The pink stripe sofa has a loose cover, practical when there are five dogs roaming around the house, and the cupboards have been cleverly disguised by wallpapering them in with the walls.

The second main guest bedroom overlooks the garden side and faces west. This also has a Colefax & Fowler chintz in the bedroom in yellows and greens and the en-suite bathroom has one of our Spencer-Churchill Designs fabrics and wallpapers, *Bladon*, a small leaf design used in the green colourway.

Next door to these two rooms is a tiny single bedroom which can also double up as a man's dressing room. There was no room for any built-in cupboards so hanging space has been created behind the curtains on the wall adjacent to the window. On the next floor up there are two attic rooms with dormer windows and a bathroom in between.

The whole house has a very inviting atmosphere and each room is full of individual character. It was and still is a house that greatly influenced me and taught me a great deal about detail, not only in the decorative sense but also in the practical sense of creating a house to suit a lifestyle.

HODGES BARN

LEFT *Irish yews and green topiary draw the eye to the front door and frame the domes of the house which was converted from a 15th-century barn and a huge dovecote.*

ABOVE *The grassed terrace on the south side of the house is a sun trap and it is here that meals are taken outside, weather permitting.*

ABOVE RIGHT *The water gardens are planted with water-loving plants and shrubs. The gardens at Hodges Barn are open to the public at various times of the year under the National Gardens Scheme.*

This attractive house was converted in 1938 by Lawrence Metheun from the original barn and columbarium, a giant dovecote. The barn dates from 1499 and was used as the store for the farm wagons for the main house. The main house, which was located next to the barn, was burned down around 1556.

The setting is idyllic. The house is approached across an open field with a drive running through the middle and glimpsed through the trees and hedges with the domes of the dovecote standing proudly as towers.

The property was bought in 1948 by my maternal great grandmother since when the internal structure has changed very little but the garden has continued to develop under the skills of my uncle Charlie Hornby and his wife Amanda.

The house is well laid out with generous yet manageable proportions. The entrance is on the north side through the front door into an inner hallway and through to the main hall. The hall, although not wide, gives the impression of being a room by the way it has been furnished. The floor is stone flags with insets of black slate. The main staircase dominates and is a mixture of stripped and painted pine. The walls are painted in yellow and the woodwork dragged in a mustard colour. The two inset painted panels are Dutch and brought from Holland by my great grandmother

LEFT *The present hall was once the central section of the barn where waggons trundled through from front to back and the long ladders were stored.*

BELOW LEFT *The tapestry hedge is very old. It is alternately planted with beech, holly and cypress.*

RIGHT *The hall is furnished very much as a room. The old oak chest is Dutch, as are the paintings.*

OVERLEAF LEFT *The main dining room was originally part of the hall, and it is furnished as a hall when it is not being used. The chairs are Dutch, and the round, cross-banded table is English.*

OVERLEAF RIGHT *The magnificent doors that lead from the main dining room to the grassed terrace.*

who was of Dutch origin. The oil portrait is of a Dutch ancestor. The oak chest forms a focal point at the base of the staircase and is an ideal place for a flower arrangement or plant.

The dining room, which leads off the hall, was originally part of the hall but my uncle and aunt required a separate dining room so they put up a partition wall and inserted the double doors leaving the vista through to the garden. When not being used for dining, the room is furnished as a hall with the round table adorned

with coffee table books and a flower arrangement.

The walls are papered in a Colefax & Fowler wallpaper and matching border which makes an ideal background for the plates. These are Angoulême and were given to one of my great grand-mother's ancestors who happened to be Mayor of The Hague when Napoleon entered the city. They are stamped with the family's crest in the centre. The other plates are French, Sèvres. The inset oil over the fireplace is again a Dutch painting. The Portuguese needlepoint rug sits on the parquet floor and was made especially in Portugal for the room, along with many other rugs in the house.

The drawing room also leads off the hall and is a light sunny room facing south and west. The curtains were recently replaced using two Charles Hammond fabrics. The outer curtains and pel-mets are fixed dress curtains and the inner ones, which draw back behind the outer ones, are pulled at night. The colour scheme is greens, yellows and reds taken from the existing Portuguese needlepoint rug. The walls are stippled in a warm yellow which offsets both the Dutch painted furniture and the glowing patina of the antique wooden pieces.

The remainder of the downstairs consists of a family kitchen with a cosy breakfast area and a family sitting room, originally a nursery housing the television.

Upstairs the main bedroom is decorated predominantly in pinks using Colefax & Fowler fabrics and wallpapers. The room was decorated around the Aubusson rug. The patchwork double wedding ring quilt bedspread was made specially in America to go in the room and my aunt sent out cuttings of the furnishing fabrics being used. The fireplace, housing a gas log fire makes a good focal point and the mixture of painted and wooden antique furniture gives the room atmosphere. The floral watercolours were painted by my grandmother, Nicole Hornby, and give a springlike, country feel to the room.

The four-poster bed in my cousin Camilla's bedroom used to belong to my aunt and the bedhangings are over 30 years old. The side tables are Portuguese and handpainted with floral motifs; the watercolours are again painted by my grandmother.

ABOVE *The lovely muted colours of the main bedroom were taken from the Aubusson carpet.*

PREVIOUS PAGE *The colour scheme in the drawing room was inspired by the Portuguese needlepoint rug. Because there are so many large windows in the room, the outer dress curtains are in a plain green self-patterned chintz which blends in well with the muted colours and the inner curtains, which are drawn at night, are in the same Charles Hammond chintz as the sofa.*

RIGHT *My cousin Camilla's bedroom is pretty and fresh with a pretty striped wallpaper that incorporates tiny flowers teamed with a floral frieze at cornice level. The painted furniture is from northern Portugal.*

BELOW *Two watercolours by my maternal grandmother, Nicole Hornby.*

PUSEY HOUSE

Pusey House is located in the Oxfordshire (formerly Berkshire) village of Pusey which lies at the foot of the Berkshire downs and close to Buckland village. It was built in about 1753 for the Pusey family. It is thought that one of the family still haunts the place.

It was bought by my maternal grandparents, Mr and Mrs Michael Hornby, in 1935 for £6,000 and this sum included most of the village consisting of some 10 cottages and about 100 acres.

The house is Georgian in style and built from stone. Internally the rooms are graced with elegant proportions. Although a fairly grand house in terms of size and decoration it always had an extremely welcoming atmosphere, even to a child. My grandmother had considerable artistic flair in many areas. She was a gifted watercolourist and she painted many of the beautiful

Pusey House, a Georgian stone manor house which was bought by my maternal grandparents along with the adjoining village. This is a view of the back as seen from across the lake.

The lake runs the length of the garden. It is a narrow lake with an island in the middle that adds a wonderful dimension to the gardens, reflecting the trees and plants that surround it.

flowers she picked from the garden as well as landscapes from various places they visited. She and my grandfather spent many hours a day toiling in the garden creating one of the most attractive gardens in England – a garden which is, in fact, open to the public. The house was beautifully maintained and run and fresh flowers and plants from the garden were displayed with enormous talent.

The entrance to the house is up a gravel drive to the east side which is somewhat austere and grey especially on a dull day. Fortunately upon entering the hall, which is raised from ground level, the atmosphere changes instantly. From the front door you look west towards the French doors which lead to the garden and lake and beyond towards the downs and you sense a marvellous feeling of depth and space. The entrance hall is furnished as a room with a working fireplace and Portuguese rug laid over a stone floor. The drawing room on the south end of the house

ABOVE *The gardens at Pusey are world famous and pictures of them have appeared in many gardening books. There is colour all year round in the wide herbaceous borders and here they are seen at their summer best.*

RIGHT *The charm of Pusey gardens lies in the delightful mixture of formal and informal, of wild and cultivated. There are areas of walled gardens, some, like this one, with delightful ornamental gateways and massed banks of colour everywhere.*

FAR RIGHT *A typical English country border planted with pink penstemon in the foreground, a yellow yarrow to the right and tall, pink mallow against the old stone wall. To the left of the gate is a climbing rose and through the gate, a clump of filipendula.*

runs off the hall and occupies the depth of the house with windows facing east and west.

The decoration has changed very little over the years and I remember spending many happy hours sitting with my grandfather at the grand piano singing nursery rhymes in the same setting then as now. It was the venue of many family get-togethers especially at Christmas.

My grandmother's sitting room runs off the drawing room facing west over the garden. The walls are painted in a blue drag which in a dark room could give a cold appearance but being a west-facing, sunny and light room the atmosphere is one of warmth. It was always a very friendly, personal room with family photographs and her watercolours dotted around the various tables and walls.

Opposite my grandmother's sitting room was my grandfather's study which was a complete contrast to her sitting room, decorated as it was in the typical style of a country gentleman's study with dark walls and dark curtains. One wall opposite the windows is lined with bookshelves housing many first editions from the family printing press. My grandfather was an avid reader so spent the hours while not in the garden reading or solving another crossword.

The dining room, one of my favourite rooms, also faces west and is painted in a stunning coral-red – a colour highly suitable for rooms used largely at night. Inset into panels are four oil

paintings of Dutch origin depicting country scenes.

The garden stretches the length of the lake which is a long nar-row, shallow lake with a small island almost opposite the centre of the house. A distinctive Chinese bridge crosses the lake south of the island and leads towards the charming little church, built in 1748 in the classical style, on the borders of the estate.

The large garden is divided into many areas both formal and rough. Running in front of the house below the terrace there is a long, deep herbacious border with well-established plants. Behind this there are several walled gardens starting with the swimming pool, which has a little pink-painted pavilion. Next to this is a large walled area housing the tennis court, kitchen garden and more flower beds and next to this is a shaped rose garden.

My grandparents have now moved from Pusey, and the house will soon be changing hands, but the garden remains as a testi-mony to their enthusiasm and their style.

ABOVE *Lady Emily's Garden, a beautiful old walled garden that was built at about the same time as the house. In the background is a little temple that houses a statue of a member of the original Pusey family, dated 1759. The garden is filled with roses, clematis and magnolia.*

RIGHT *The lake at Pusey is a shallow one with clumps of lilies and other water-loving plants growing in and around it. The bridge, which leads to a gravel path and eventually to the church, was built in the Chinese Chippendale style.*

Cornwell Manor

This house is, in my view, along with Lee Place, one of the most attractive houses in Oxfordshire. It is a low gabled house, built around three-and-a-half sides of a courtyard. My cousins live here and as well as having a lot in common with one another, we were at school together in Oxford and shared the school run, so I spent a lot of time here as a child.

It is not only the house that is so appealing but its location and surroundings. The house sits on a hill overlooking the gardens and is the manor house of the village, or more, correctly, the hamlet, of Cornwell. The cottages and buildings of the village are again built on a hillside, sloping down to a stream and village green. They have been modernized over the years but mostly date from the 17th century.

Parts of the house are thought to date back as far as early medieval times. This has come to light from old plans of the cellars and the remaining semi-circular staircase located to the west of the dining room. The core of the house is 16th and 17th century.

The oldest remaining features are the Jacobean panelling in the dining room and library. The existing main hall and dining room are the nucleus of the original house to which additions have been grafted on from time to time.

Most of the additions were made by the Penystone family who lived there for three centuries. The first additions forming the courtyard were made in about 1640, and the later Georgian additions, notably the front facade, were added in about 1750.

The house was restored again in 1939 by Clough Williams-Ellis for the Gibson family. They added the ballroom to the north-east side and they remodelled the entrance hall to imitate a courtyard with arches around the walls and rusticated doorways. The stone fireplace in the hall is 18th century and is decorated with the Penystone Arms. The main staircase is Georgian with turned balusters and carved treads and the staircase hall has a coved ceiling and bracket cornice and a Venetian window. The drawing room, to the right of the main hall, has an Adam style fireplace and two built-in mirrors on the opposite wall with rococo plasterwork frames.

The gardens were also formally laid out at this time by Clough Williams-Ellis, who terraced the valley south of the house and canalized the stream into an artificial pool. Formal steps lead down to it on both sides and on to a gateway through which there is a magnificent vista towards the facade of the house. The main drive is just to the west of this gateway, over a small bridge with an artifically created cascade.

The present owners have, over a period of some 35 years, redecorated the rooms to keep in line with current trends yet clearly managing to retain the architectural features.

The main entrance brings you into the hall, which in this case could be properly described as a room rather than an area to pass through. It has been furnished as a room and is certainly large enough to be one, creating an inviting atmosphere as you first enter the house. The colour scheme is predominantly red and green which adds to the feeling of warmth. The arches were painted to look like stone and the rest of the woodwork is dragged in a soft beige – both these finishes were expertly carried out by the owner herself. The curtains, which have been hanging some 30 years, have swags and tails edged in a red bullion fringe which links the curtain fabric to the walls. The two sofas are upholstered in a green linen, contrast-piped in red, with scatter cushions of a Colefax & Fowler fabric, *Pansies and Roses*. This chintz, which blends very well with the old curtain chintz, is also

ABOVE *One of four lead statues that are dotted around the garden.*

ABOVE RIGHT *Looking towards the stable block and garages from the west, a view that shows the glorious variety of shrubs in the garden.*

OVERLEAF *The drawing room is a wonderfully elegant room with a colour scheme based on the magnificent Aubusson rug in rich and welcoming shades of cream, pink and red.*

PAGE 58 *The study, which leads off the drawing room is also decorated in reds and pinks to achieve a feeling of cosiness as well as a flow of colour throughout the downstairs rooms. Individually, the dog paintings are nothing special but together they make a definite impression.*

PAGE 59 *Looking into the inviting glow of the study from the garden.*

used to upholster the two extremely comfortable armchairs.

The floor has the original flagstones, which over the years have built up a wonderful patina. A rug of rush matting sits on top of these to define the seating area in front of the fire. Apart from the small lantern overhead, all the lighting is indirect. Table lamps provide a soft warm feel at night reflecting the red of the walls.

Used mainly for entertaining, the more formal drawing room has a colour scheme centred around the magnificent Aubusson rug in shades of cream, gold and crimson. The walls are panelled with plaster mouldings and painted in a soft rag finish in a champagne colour. The mouldings have been painted to match, with some areas left white to give a contrast. The skirting is the original wood plank.

The dress curtains and their magnificent swag and tail pelmets are hung from plaster pelmets. The fabric, a pink linen called *toile Penelope*, is edged with a linen fringe and fan edge in pink and white. At night the striped silk festoon curtains are let down. The two sofas are covered in a cut velvet stripe with a wool bullion fringe around the base and the two armchairs are in a Colefax & Fowler chintz. There is no overhead lighting, only table lamps, which again create soft, warm pools of light.

The red sitting room is next door to the drawing room and is entered through a cupboard used as a bar. The colour scheme follows through well. It is a cosy spot housing the television and an open fire and is designed to be used as a family room. The walls

are papered in a Colefax & Fowler design with a border to frame the walls. The dado rail has been left white but below this the walls have been painted in a wild stipple finish and the skirting marbleized. The doors and frames have been dragged and again all the specialist paintwork was done by the owner. The sofa is covered in a cut velvet stripe, with a red wool bullion fringe around the skirt. The assortment of cushions breaks the solid colour of velvet and picks out the other colours used in the room. Above the two painted wheelback chairs is an assortment of oil paintings of dogs. The carpet was made by Bosanquet & Ives and is a cut pile patterned carpet with a border.

The dining room faces over the inner courtyard so it is not a very light room and gives off a much more sombre and older feel than the other main rooms of the house. This is largely due to the original Jacobean panelling. The grey, feathery hand painting on the panelling is undoubtedly old, it was found under several coats of paint during restoration work.

The curtains have been hanging for some time. They are a Colefax & Fowler self-patterned linen in a lime green. The carpet, which was replaced more recently is a Brussels weave in a

diagonal design with a *fleur de lys* border in greens and pinks. The dining chairs are Sheraton, in mahogany, as is the dining table which at night is generally covered with a white linen cloth. The side cabinets are bamboo and lacquer and stand out well against the feathered panelling.

The main upstairs rooms are approached via a large winding staircase leading from the inner hall. The main bedroom is at the end, facing over the gardens and lake beyond. It has been recently redecorated in pinks and whites using fabrics especially printed by Bernard Thorp. The walls are painted in a soft pink eggshell finish and on either side of the bed hang portraits of the owner's two sons drawn by Charmian Stirling. Round tables with fabric cloths are used as bedside tables. The bedspread was purchased locally in an antique shop and on the reverse side it has a pink quilted design. The cushions are antique lace. Over the bed hangs a fine example of a fabric corona using the curtain fabric on the outside and the contrast fabric on the inside.

The two main guest bedrooms both have four-poster beds. The blue bedroom remains little changed over the last 25 years and is simple, fresh and elegant in style. The four-poster, hanging

wardrobe, three window pelmets, long mirror and chaise longue were all purchased for next to nothing. They are late 18th century, painted in black and gold and the blue silk curtains and bed hangings make a stunning contrast. The pelmets are edged in a cream silk fringe and the same blue has been used for the round tablecloths and to frame the beautiful appliqué bedspread. The panels of the cupboard are lined in a pleated blue silk and the inside of the bed hangings are lined in cream silk. Two blue and cream rugs break up the expanse of beige carpet and a touch of pattern has recently been added in the form of the Colefax & Fowler *Plumbago Bouquet* chintz on the armchair and chaise longue. The walls are wallpapered in a damask-type design in cream and white which gives a warmer feel to the room than plain painted walls would give. Even the most unobstrusive patterned surfaces have the effect of adding depth to a room.

The second guest room is yellow and green and is much more vibrant in contrast. The colour scheme centres around an old Warner's chintz with lots of flowers and leaves, the walls are painted yellow and the soft furnishings picked out in a similar colour. The four-poster bed was sent over by a friend of the family from the Bahamas and is unusual in that it has polished mahogany posts and a painted cornice.

The whole atmosphere of this house reflects classic English comfort and style at its best, exuding the warmth and welcome of a well-loved home.

ABOVE LEFT *The main bedroom has recently been redecorated, the theme taken from the pink and cream printed cotton fabric.*

ABOVE *The main guest bedroom is a lovely sunny room with windows on three sides. The curtains and bed hangings are in blue and cream silk.*

RIGHT *Another view of the blue bedroom showing the appliqué bedspread and the armchair and chaise, recently re-upholstered in a Colefax & Fowler chintz.*

PREVIOUS PAGE LEFT *Guest bedroom decorated in light and sunny greens and yellows around the beautiful old chintz curtains.*

PREVIOUS PAGE RIGHT *The wood panelled dining room looks over an internal courtyard. It looks wonderful by day and by night.*

BLENHEIM PRIVATE AND PUBLIC

Blenheim was a gift bestowed on John Churchill, First Duke of Marlborough, by Queen Anne to serve as a triumphant monument to Marlborough's victory over the French at the battle of Blenheim. The Palace, was to be sited within the grounds of the Royal Woodstock Park, now called Blenheim Park. The architect John Vanbrugh was commissioned to design and build this historic monument and it was he who, with Marlborough, chose the actual location within the Park.

Work commenced on the foundations in 1705 and Vanbrugh and Marlborough worked closely together to produce primarily a monument, secondly a home. It was to be built from east to west, so that the Duke and his Duchess, Sarah, could move into their private apartments in the East Wing as soon as possible.

The resulting Palace is one of the greatest examples of English baroque architecture and superb craftsmanship. Vanbrugh was assisted in his great work by Nicholas Hawksmoor who had studied under Wren and together they selected the

The Duchess's Sitting Room is in the private wing overlooking the Italian Gardens.

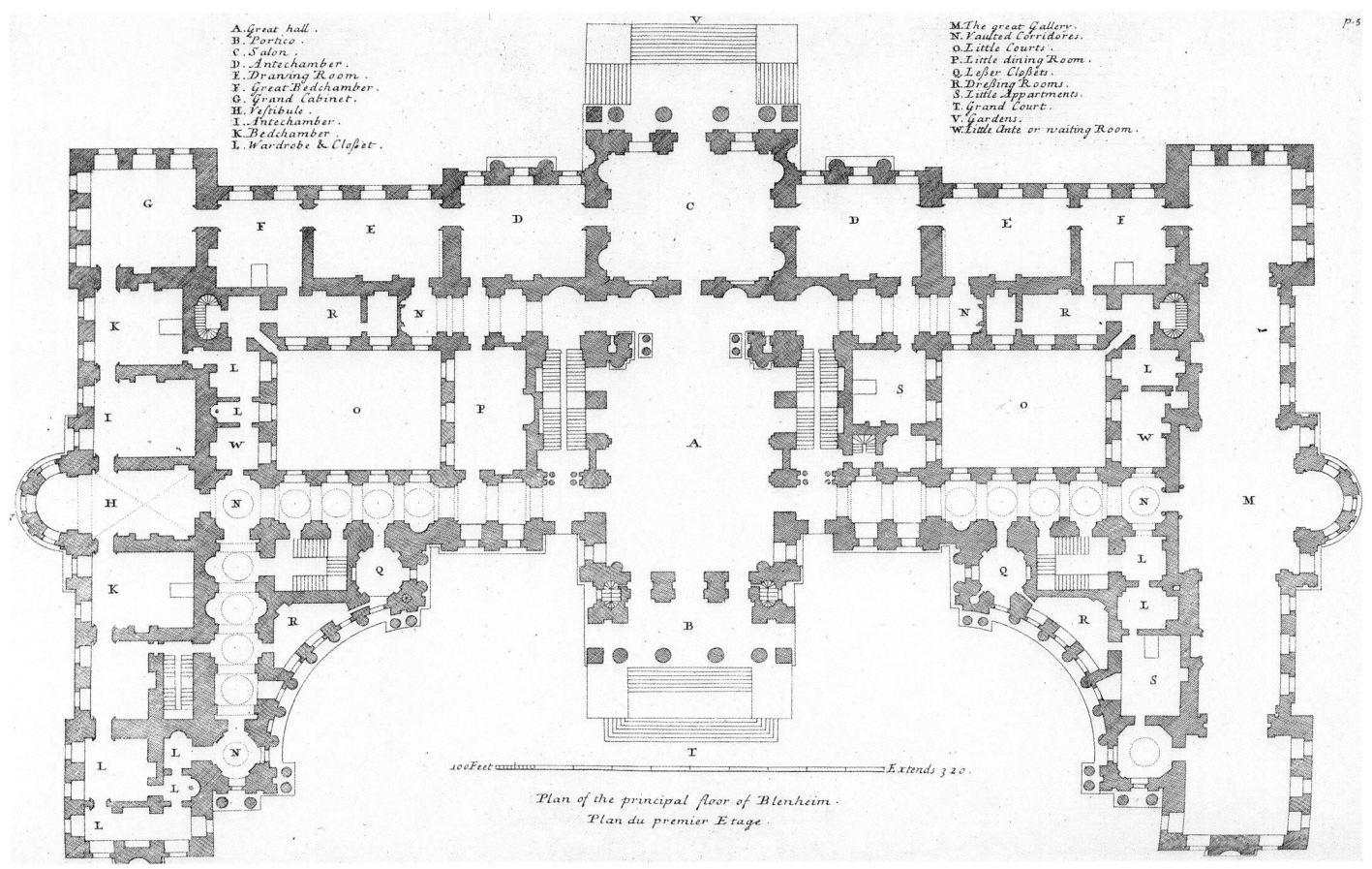

A. Great hall.
B. Portico.
C. Salon.
D. Antechamber.
E. Drawing Room.
F. Great Bedchamber.
G. Grand Cabinet.
H. Vestibule.
I. Antechamber.
K. Bedchamber.
L. Wardrobe & Closet.

M. The great Gallery.
N. Vaulted Corridores.
O. Little Courts.
P. Little dining Room.
Q. Lesser Closets.
R. Dressing Rooms.
S. Little Appartments.
T. Grand Court.
V. Gardens.
W. Little Ante or waiting Room.

Plan of the principal floor of Blenheim.
Plan du premier Etage.

Plan of the principal floor of Blenheim Palace, 1717, as inscribed by Colin Campbell in Volume I of Vitruvius Britannicus.

most gifted craftsmen of the age including master masons Edward Strong, John Townsend, Bartholomew Peisley and Henry Banks. Grinling Gibbons was responsible for most of the stone carving and ornamentation internally and externally, including 22 statues.

A QUESTION OF COSTS

The artist Sir James Thornhill was commissioned to paint the ceiling in the Great Hall. He chose to depict Marlborough dressed as a Roman general showing the plan of the battle of Blenheim to Britannia, and all for 25 shillings a yard. Sarah considered this far too expensive and in a cost-cutting exercise, James Thornhill's plans for the adjoining Saloon were abandoned and Louis Laguerre was chosen to paint the ceiling and murals partly because his quote was more competitive at a mere £500.

Costs were to prove a contentious issue throughout. Vanbrugh was not Queen Anne's choice of architect. She favoured Christopher Wren, but Marlborough had chosen Vanbrugh. As the Palace was to be built at the royal expense, Queen Anne was

ABOVE *The architect: Sir John Vanbrugh 1664–1726, painted by Murray c. 1718. Vanbrugh led a colourful life outside architecture. He was arrested as a spy in France and spent some time languishing in the Bastille. He was the author of several successful Restoration comedies, his best known being* The Provoked Wife *(1697).*

ABOVE RIGHT *The clients: The 1st Duke and Duchess of Marlborough with their children, painted by Closterman.*

naturally nervous when Vanbrugh failed to come up with an estimate. Wren looked admiringly over his colleague's plans and estimated a total cost of £100,000. The final reckoning was nearer £300,000, to which Marlborough was obliged to contribute £60,000 of his own. Queen Anne stopped paying the bills in 1712 when she finally fell out with the remarkable Sarah.

Blenheim Palace was finally completed in 1722, the year the Duke died, but Vanbrugh had abandoned the project in 1716 after numerous arguments with Sarah. In 1719 the Duke and Duchess were able to move into the East Wing, but the Duke by then had barely two summers left in which to enjoy his national gift.

THE FORMAL GARDENS

While the Palace was under construction, great attention was being given to the gardens and the landscaping of the park. Vanbrugh always saw the two developing together, and it was he who designed the Grand Bridge to span the River Glyme and create an important approach to the house. The great gardener Henry Wise was commissioned to lay out the formal gardens. He was responsible for the two main avenues of elms to the east and north, now sadly destroyed by Dutch elm disease. Wise's brief was to create an instant garden and park which Marlborough, who was a sick man, could enjoy before his death.

At the time of the Duke's death, the Chapel at Blenheim was still not complete, but his body finally came to rest there many years later in the great tomb designed by William Kent.

Following her husband's death, Sarah continued to complete

Watercolours by Susan Blandford, wife of the philandering 5th Duke who succeeded in 1817 and was forced to sell off Blenheim's splendid library in order to pay his debts.

Blenheim and instructed Nicholas Hawksmoor to return in 1722. He produced designs for the Triumphal Arch at the town entrance to the park, completed the decoration of the Chapel, the Gallery (now called the Long Library) and various other ceilings and ornamental features for the house. Sarah lived in Blenheim until her death in 1744 and at the age of 80 made an inventory of Blenheim down to the last napkin (there were 809) and the number of servants' sheets (45 pairs). The terms of her will stated that on no account was the Palace to be denuded of its contents.

EXPENSES MOUNT UP

In 1733 Charles Spencer succeeded as 3rd Duke of Marlborough and after his grandmother's death he lived intermittently at Blenheim. He did very little to add to the splendour of the house and gardens other than commission a few portraits of his family. George, his eldest son, succeeded to the Dukedom aged 19 in 1758 by which time most of the rooms were furnished. The 4th Duke was the first member of the family to use Blenheim as a permanent home. He turned the Orangery into a private theatre, and entertained lavishly and often. He was responsible for many expensive additions to Blenheim both internally and externally. He commissioned Lancelot (Capability) Brown to relandscape the Park. Brown's most spectacular creation was the great lake spreading between the valley of the River Glyme and spanned by Vanbrugh's great bridge. He planted trees in casual clumps and grassed over Henry Wise's formal 'military' garden to the south. He was also responsible for transforming High Lodge, a hunting lodge, into a gothic toy castle.

George, the 4th Duke, the Duchess Caroline and their family painted by Reynolds in 1778.

Meanwhile, additional work on the house was being carried out by Sir William Chambers, the architect responsible for Somerset House and, incidently, the design of the Royal State Coach. He added embellishments externally and decorated rooms inside. He was responsible for the building of various temples within the garden and for the New Bridge over the Glyme on the side of the Park near to the village of Bladon.

SELLING THE HEIRLOOMS

The 5th Duke, the first duke to take the name Spencer-Churchill, succeeded in 1817. He was a great botanist and was determined to create 'the finest botanical and flower garden in England', but he fell heavily in debt and not only did he fail to finish his magical garden, he also was forced to sell his great library to appease the bailiffs. He was a spendthrift and a philanderer and his poor Duchess, Susan, had plenty of time on her hands. Her legacy was a portfolio of exquisite flower paintings which is now kept in the Long Library. The 6th Duke likewise did little to embellish or

69

maintain Blenheim, except to open it to the public at the highly unrealistic sum of five shillings, reduced to one after an outcry.

John Spencer-Churchill, the 7th Duke, was a generous and hospitable man. He was forced to keep up appearances at Blenheim on a very tight budget. In 1875 he sold off family jewels to pay debts and in 1881 he sold one of Blenheim's primary treasures, the Sunderland Library which had been put together by the bookish Charles Spencer, father of the 3rd Duke, and hailed as the greatest collection of books ever assembled. He was able to do this only because in 1880, the Marlborough heirlooms lost their protected status. This opened the floodgates. The 8th Duke continued selling Blenheim's great treasures despite protests from his brother, Lord Randolph Churchill, the father of the great Sir Winston. But at least the money was put to good use, developing the farms and modernising Blenheim internally.

THE AMERICAN COLLECTION

The 8th Duke made a fortunate second marriage to a wealthy American, Lilian Hammersley, and with her help he was actually able to add some historic legacies, the most notable being the Willis organ in the Long Library, the boathouse and the much appreciated central heating. In spite of this last-minute buying spree, when Charles 9th Duke of Marlborough succeeded in 1892 he found Blenheim stripped of many of its heirlooms and he and his wealthy American wife, Consuelo Vanderbilt, set about restoring the Palace and its grounds. Charles employed the French architect Achille Duchêne to restore the formal gardens that Capability Brown had grassed over, he brought over Parisian craftsmen to decorate three of the state rooms in the ornate and gilded French style and he started re-stocking the Long Library.

The First World War interrupted the rebuilding programme. The Long Library was turned into a hospital ward and part of the South Lawn was planted with potatoes. By the time the war was over, Charles and Consuelo had parted company, rather acrimoniously, and Gladys Deacon was installed as the new Duchess. 'Sunny' as he was nicknamed – deriving from the title The Earl of Sunderland – was a perfectionist. He took endless pains with the Water Terrace Gardens, which were the cause of many arguments with Duchêne, and then he decided that he disliked the French decoration he had commissioned for the Salons, but was persuaded to leave it. 'Sunny' died in 1934, having spent some wonderful years at Blenheim, both restoring it and entertaining grandly within its splendid walls.

ABOVE *Charles, the 9th Duke, his wife the former Consuelo Vanderbilt and their family painted by Sargent.*

OVERLEAF LEFT *The bookcases in the Long Library showing the detailed plasterwork mouldings picked out in white against the peachy-coloured walls.*

OVERLEAF RIGHT *Detail of the bookshelves, showing a selection of leather-bound volumes. The books cover every subject from Antiques to Zoology and the library is used by scholars and librarians from all over the world.*

WAR AND THE AFTERMATH

My grandfather 'Bert', the 10th Duke, moved into Blenheim with his wife, Mary Cadogan, in 1920. My grandmother immediately set about turning Blenheim into a home, greatly improving the amenities (there was only one bathroom when she moved in) and enhancing the atmosphere. The house became alive with children and dogs running around the corridors and the grounds were full of energetic youngsters on their bicycles or on horseback. There were shooting parties, garden parties and house parties on a grand scale, the highlight being my Aunt Sarah's coming out ball in July 1939. There were a thousand guests and the party was talked about for many years as it came to symbolize the last bright summer of peace. By September, England was once again at war, and life would never be the same.

Within months Blenheim was being blacked out for the Second World War. The Long Library was turned into an overcrowded dormitory for 400 Malvern College boys, the Great Hall was used as a dining room and the whole house was covered with matting and linoleum. The boys were there for a year and they were followed by MI5, members of the British Council and the

Ministry of Supply. The family retreated to the privacy of the East Wing, abandoning the State Rooms to the British Government, and later to the people. After the war the Ministry of Works lent a hand in the long process of restoring Blenheim in preparation for opening it to the public. On the 1st April, 1950, the doors were first opened at a charge of half-a-crown a head. The first day 230 people appeared and the numbers of visitors rose quickly to 100,000 a year.

Thanks to Vanbrugh's original layout, it was quite possible for the family to reside in the East Wing while visitors traipsed around the State Rooms. The revenue helped towards the enormous upkeep costs but it was not enough. Work was constantly being carried out and much of its on the crumbling stonework. To raise revenue, certain rooms were let out for conferences.

My grandfather created his own private garden which became one of his passions along with his love of shooting. It was located to the south east, easily accessible from the house down a private staircase leading from the Sitting Room down to the South Lawn. It was begun in 1954 and was a wild romantic garden, largely English in style though influenced by 18th-century Italian Gardens.

After my grandmother died in 1961 the atmosphere at Blenheim was melancholy and without her dedication and perfectionism in running the household, it lacked love. My grandfather continued to live there until his death in 1972, working on his garden and entertaining his guests at shooting parties.

THE PRESENT DAY

By the time my father succeeded in 1972, he already had a good deal of experience in running Blenheim and his own farm. In 1953, after he had married my mother (formerly Susan Hornby now married to John Gough) he bought Lee Place, a lovely Georgian farmhouse, which was the home in which my brother James and I were brought up.

In the spring of 1972, my father married Rosita Douglas and together they moved into Blenheim, determined to restore it to the family home it once was and dispel the neglected, austere air it had developed since my grandmother's death. It was my father's view that it was necessary to live on the spot, firstly to create the desired atmosphere and secondly to keep it going. If Blenheim was to survive as a privately-owned historic house, then the enthusiasm to live in it had to be there, along with the determination to make it pay for its upkeep.

RIGHT *The Third State Room, next to the Long Library. When all the doors are open, you can look from one end of the South Wing to the other. You are supposed to be able to see through even when the doors are shut, because the keyholes line up exactly. Tapestries and paintings dominate all the State Rooms.*

OVERLEAF LEFT *Marble and gilt table in the Saloon. It has a flagstone floor inset with marble squares and the walls are of stone. The candelabra is electrified now, but was originally designed to take candles. The room is used by the family for dinner every Christmas night.*

OVERLEAF RIGHT *The Duke's Dressing Room overlooks the Italian gardens. It is a very smart and masculine room with beige suede battened onto the walls and an Empire day bed upholstered in a periwinkle blue linen.*

In order to make Blenheim an attractive and practical venue for both private and business entertaining, it needed a massive face-lift. My stepmother, who is extremely artistic and has very good taste, supervised the changes which were carried out with great sensitivity over a long period of time.

Although we did not live at Blenheim all year round (the summer months were, and still are, spent at Lee Place) Blenheim soon became a home with a very warm and inviting atmosphere despite the vast proportions of the rooms. But the layout is not at all practical for the lives we live today. For example, the kitchen is on a floor below the Dining Room and there is a long walk from the pantry, where the food first arrives from the kitchen, to the Dining Room. That the food is still hot when it is finally wheeled in is no mean tribute to the skills of the chef!

THE STUDY AND THE DUKE'S DRESSING ROOM

The main living accommodation in the private East Wing is located on the first floor as opposed to the ground floor. Part of the ground floor is located below ground level and part is at ground level. This is due to the varying levels of the terraces and

76

gardens outside, and it can sometimes be very confusing. There are fewer rooms than you would imagine, all of which are comfortably decorated and welcoming.

My father's wood-panelled study is located in the north-east corner of the East Wing. Its windows, framed with heavy velvet curtains, look over the North Courtyard on one side and the Italian Gardens on the other. It has changed very little since my grandfather's day and still houses many of his personal mementoes. It has never been open to public view, and it is one of my favourite rooms.

Next door to the study, accessible by a connecting double door (two doors with cupboard space in between, found in most of the rooms at Blenheim) is my father's dressing room. This overlooks the Italian Gardens and is a light, sunny room. The decoration is masculine with a beige suede on the walls (selected by my stepmother and myself with my father's approval) which provides an excellent background for pictures. The curtains are a café-au-lait linen and the room is furnished in Empire style with an Empire day bed covered in blue linen with beige braiding and two chairs by Jacob with their original canvas. The whole effect is very becoming indeed and, I think, typical of an English country gentleman's retreat.

MASTER BEDROOM AND BATHROOMS

Off the dressing room, again approached though a set of double doors, is the Master Bedroom which is a spacious, well-proportioned room with a very high ceiling, appropriately housing a magnificent 18th-century four-poster bed. The room was refurbished in 1974 by my stepmother with the help of interior decorators Lenygon & Morant. The bed was painted and the original silk brocade bed curtains and hangings were re-vamped to improve their proportions with the addition of a Colefax & Fowler fabric called *Hollyhock*. The chairs and chaise longue were also covered in *Hollyhock*, giving the room a less formal air. Their bathroom is opposite the bedroom and adjacent to the dressing room. It is an internal room converted by my grandfather from a lobby area and it has no window. It was originally a long narrow room with a very high ceiling and felt like a dark tunnel. My stepmother divided the room in two to provide a separate guest cloakroom, lowered the ceiling, added a large mirror and created a much more inviting environment.

The original bathroom, installed in the 1890's, is across the passage and it still has its old-fashioned fittings with a wooden

loo located behind a door, a free-standing marble-topped wash basin and old-fashioned towel rails. The only modern addition is my father's jacuzzi bath, to help ease the aches and pains from many hours in the saddle. My grandfather installed a Turkish bath for much the same reasons, but this has since been removed.

THE DUCHESS'S DINING ROOM

The Dining Room, originally called The Bow Window Room was one of Sarah, 1st Duchess of Marlborough's favourite rooms. The chimneypiece was carved by Grinling Gibbons along with the frieze and the Corinthian capitals. The bow is furnished with two gilt and marble console tables with two pier glasses by the gifted cabinetmaker James Moore hung between the arched windows. The curtains are in a cream silk damask with swagged pelmets shaped to follow the elegant arch and trimmed with a silk fringe and rope. The original curtains were too short and are now hung on seven-inch chains concealed behind the pelmets.

At the other end of the room the walls are covered with three tapestry panels depicting the Arts of War, a series commissioned by the 1st Duke. For small numbers of people, a round table is placed in the bow window and for larger numbers· the table extends to the appropriate length. A painted screen sits in front of the double doors leading to the passage, which conveniently shields the dining guests from the butler and vice versa.

The room was painted about 15 years ago by Brian Beelan, a

ABOVE LEFT *Over the windows in the Duchess's Dining Room a stiff band, decorated with rosettes, has been formed to follow the arch and the pelmets fall from that. The Venetian curtains pull back on a drawstring so they draw back without cutting out any light. A roller blind attached to the window can be pulled down to stop the sunlight rotting the furnishings.*

ABOVE *Candles provide the main source of light in the evenings. The candelabra are placed in front of the mirrors to reflect the light.*

RIGHT *The Dining Room is used purely for private functions. It can be used with a large table running down the centre of the room, or with a small table in the bay window.*

PREVIOUS PAGE *The Master Bedroom with its magnificent painted bed and silk curtains.*

The Smoking Room is the everyday sitting room. The incredibly deep sofa seats five people in comfort, it would overwhelm an ordinary sitting room. The old green leather armchair in the foreground was my grandfather's favourite chair and it is now my father's favourite. The walls are lined with a warm coral linen and the room is dominated by the enormous Le Brun tapestry depicting the Triumph of Alexander.

well-known and talented specialist painter. The walls were dragged and stippled in much the same way as they would have been painted originally. The panelling was dragged and the edges picked out in soft shades of yellow, apricot and grey, the grey being the contrast to the yellow which highlights the mouldings. The pillars came in for the same treatment to accentuate their mouldings and carvings. The colours have been kept deliberately pale and soft to reflect light into the room. It is here that the Christmas tree is erected. Standing 16 foot tall in the bow window it is a magnificent sight.

THE SMOKING ROOM

Next to the Dining Room is the Smoking Room. It is very much a family room, housing the television, children's books and games. Supper is eaten in here on trays or on a small table when there are just a few people and a fire glows, though sadly now it is a gas one, installed after a fire damaged the chimney.

The walls are covered in a warm coral fabric and the paintwork is a soft grey picked out in coral. My stepmother has added and changed things over the years giving it a typical country house

The Duchess's Sitting Room has recently been redecorated by my stepmother. The gilt armchairs were re-upholstered in an old-fashioned silk damask to bring out the blue tones of the carpet and complement the charming portrait by Ambrose McEvoy of Consuelo Vanderbilt Balsan after her divorce from the 9th Duke and her subsequent remarriage to a Frenchman.

feel. The one thing never to change is my grandfather's favourite green leather chair, now used by my father.

THE DUCHESS'S SITTING ROOM AND THE GRAND CABINET

Next door is the Duchess's Sitting Room, an elegant room painted in a warm yellow-gold. This has been revamped very recently by my stepmother who changed the furnishings and the layout while keeping the existing curtains and wall colours. The effect is sensational. The original curtains were re-made by Lenygon & Morant to my stepmother's design, and a silk fringe was added along with some antique silk bobbles which had been found tucked away in one of the attic rooms at Blenheim. The tiebacks were made from an old silk wall hanging.

The Grand Cabinet is located on the south-east corner. It is a much more formal room that the others and is only opened up and used when guests are staying, and then only in the evenings. It has a grand piano which sadly none of the family plays and many family portraits. Its double doors connect to the Green Drawing Room, the first room on the south side open to the public.

ABOVE *This passage leads to the main rooms on the private side. All the rooms on this floor are above ground level, so you cannot walk out into the gardens but it does mean that the rooms get more light. As much of the Palace is built round internal courtyards, the interior needs all the light it can get. The curtains are in an old-fashioned Colefax & Fowler cotton edged in a wool bullion fringe, an ideal match for the runner carpet and the paintwork. The portrait of my father at the end by the bar is by Lafontaine as is the one above the doorway, which depicts the Duke and Duchess on horseback.*

RIGHT *Stunning portrait of Consuelo Vanderbilt, the wealthy American wife of the 9th Duke, by Veruda. The portrait is the focal point of this passage overlooking the North Courtyard which leads to the Duchess's Dining Room. The soft blue of her dress is echoed in the collection of Chinese porcelain ginger jars and vases.*

LEFT *The Water Terraces at Blenheim were designed by Achille Duchêne following the principles of the famous Le Nôtre who designed the gardens of Versailles. Low box hedges clipped into elaborate scrolling patterns make for gardens that are best admired from upstairs windows.*

RIGHT *Font Room One is the romantic name of the room which was revamped by Woodstock Designs to show our new Blenheim fabric collection. We wanted to maintain the character of the room while giving it a new, updated look. We used all the existing furniture, stripping off and restoring the cornice of the mahogany four-poster. The carpet is a Brussels weave with a tiny diamond pattern that co-ordinates with the wallpaper, the matching fabric and the chintz. The design makes good use of the beautiful proportions of the room and the fresh flower-sprigged chintz brings a sunny, garden feeling into it.*

UPSTAIRS AND DOWNSTAIRS

The upstairs, or second floor, of the private wing consists mainly of guest bedrooms and seven bathrooms as well as Edward and Alexandra's rooms (my half-brother and sister), the nursery and Nanny and Ray's bedroom (our nanny married the butler). These rooms are of varying degrees of grandeur. The largest have four-poster beds and tapestries on the walls, and the smallest look quite ordinary. Many of the bathrooms were later additions, as the Palace had very little in the way of plumbing until the turn of the century, therefore only a few are en suite and are mostly internal rooms, neither large nor spectacular.

My old bedroom is up here too. Shortly after grandfather's death, when my father was planning to move in to Blenheim, my brother James and I were told we could choose (to a certain degree) which bedroom we each would like. After much deliberation we finally made our decisions and I selected a small conventional bedroom overlooking the South Lawn with spectacular light and views. My brother chose a less conventional 'den' – a tiny bedroom with another little room linked to it situated on the north-east side in between the first and second floors.

Two views of the little bedroom on the south side which was my room when I lived at Blenheim in the holidays. I chose the furnishings and the fabric myself and I still like it. The room has not been changed since I outgrew it and it is a guest bedroom now. It is still pretty and fresh and gets a lot of light thanks to the huge window which has shutters to close at night to keep out the draughts.

I was then allowed to select the curtains and wallpaper for my room and this was really the first time that I had to choose anything for myself that I would have to live with. I can remember taking the decision very seriously and giving it a lot of thought. Finally, with my stepmother's help and guidance we decided on a fabric with a white background which had a pink ribbon running vertically down in wide stripes and flowers in between in blue, pink and green. The wallpaper had a pale blue background with a slightly darker motif on top. The effect was simple and fresh and something I would still choose today.

From an exploring point of view, Blenheim is paradise. There are endless concealed staircases leading to different rooms, towers and levels between main floors. These rooms are rarely used other than for storage, but in earlier times they were staff rooms, which explains why the area is named 'Housemaid Heights'.

Blenheim is a very warm and comfortable house with a surprisingly relaxed atmosphere despite its forbidding grandeur. It is now what it was always intended to be: a national monument and a home, a real home, for the descendants of John Churchill, 1st Duke of Marlborough and his Duchess, the formidable Sarah.

LEFT *The Tower Room Bedroom is a wonderfully old-fashioned bedroom which faces south and east, looking over the Italian Gardens and the South Lawn. It is a guest bedroom with a very special atmosphere and a magnificent old four-poster with barley-sugar twist posts with old silk damask hangings. The curtains and the upholstery fabrics are all old and rare and everything exudes an air of comfort.*

ABOVE *The dressing room adjacent to the Sunderland Room, another guest bedroom, that was refurbished 15 years ago. It has red Suedel on the walls, which is a paper-backed mock suede that makes a wonderful background for gilt-framed oil paintings. The room, which has an immensely high ceiling, benefits from the rich mixture of patterns.*

THE PORTFOLIO

Woodstock Designs was founded in 1981. It is an interior design company that specializes in classic English interiors in all their manifestations. We have designed hotels in Scotland, motorcruisers in the South of France and penthouses in Manhattan but most of our work is in country houses in Oxfordshire and flats and town houses in London. I work with my partner, Zoë Westropp, my consultant designer, Ian Walton, and a small staff. Between us we handle briefs as complex as the complete renovation of a country estate to the design and decoration of a single room or a single set of curtains.

Country houses are a particular favourite of mine. Houses in the country tend to have more generous proportions than town houses. Rooms are bigger and taller, windows are larger so there's more light. There are more rooms on the same level and halls and landings are large enough to be treated as rooms rather than passageways.

Town houses pose interesting challenges too. It is like solving an intricate jig-saw puzzle, squeezing bathrooms into cupboards, turning passageways into dining rooms and trying to flood the place with natural light when you are literally up against a brick wall.

The dining room in the main house of a Cotswold farm has yellow walls to make it sunnier and brighter.

COTSWOLD FARMHOUSE

This typical Cotswold stone farmhouse dates from about 1820. It was a compact, south-facing house consisting of five bedrooms, a small sitting room, a dining room and a kitchen. Its main potential lay in the magnificent range of barns and outbuildings which form natural extensions to the main house.

Woodstock Designs were commissioned to design and decorate the interiors as the rooms were finished, and it has proved to be an ongoing job. The first room we tackled was the new large drawing room on the ground floor. It had the advantage of wonderful natural light with windows on three sides and as a focal point there was a large, open fireplace. The room was planned for formal entertaining in both summer and winter and the owners required an ambiance that was both formal yet warm and welcoming.

As the main colour theme we chose an English chintz with pink and reds and blues and greens on a printed background, and we used this fabric as a loose cover on a sofa. For the curtains we

picked an almost plain chintz with a small dot design in two tones of pink. From a distance the fabric appears plain, but close up you can distinguish the design, which gives more depth of colour than a plain fabric could. The pelmet was edged in a rope fringe of two tones of pink with a matching rope and tiebacks.

The present dining room leads off the hall which has the original flagstone floor. For the curtains the owner wanted something heavy in weight but not oppressive and settled on an Indian crewelwork fabric which I had imported from Kashmir in India. The walls are painted yellow to reflect the sunlight and give a warm glow to the room at all times.

Next door to the dining room is the kitchen which is simply equipped with an Aga stove, pine units and a free standing pine dresser on one wall. The floor has terracotta tiles which, although cold to touch, look warm. The walls are painted in an off-white which is more suitable than a brilliant white next to the old pine.

The Granary, although not attached to the main house, was the ideal building to convert into a guest area. It already had two storeys with windows – the ground floor being originally the cowshed and the upstairs the grain store. With the help of local architect Richard Waddington work started on the conversion.

Both the owner and the architect were intent on using as much antique and salvaged materials as possible to give the building an authentic look. The very attractive open conservatory was found in Scotland on a disused site and cleverly reassembled. Tops of

ABOVE LEFT *The drawing room faces south. The walls have a soft hint of pink to add warmth and provide a good background for pictures.*

ABOVE & RIGHT *The downstairs at the Granary is often used for entertaining. The benches are old pews from a church in Scotland, the murals that echo the shape of the mirror are by local artist Peter Sokolof Edwards.*

PREVIOUS PAGE LEFT *The open conservatory linking the Granary to the main house was salvaged from a disused site in Scotland.*

PREVIOUS PAGE RIGHT *The kitchen in the main house is painted off-white to complement the old pine.*

OVERLEAF *Guest bedroom and bathroom upstairs in the Granary. The theme is buttermilk and yellow with a traditional country feel.*

old gutters were used as uplighters and later a fountain was installed on the back wall. An outside staircase was created and the arched entrance to the ground floor built from old stones. The ground floor consists of one long room with a massive open fireplace at one end. The pine beams are original and all the doors used are old pine ones salvaged from a brewery. The floor consists of pine planks with rugs thrown on top. Around the fireplace is a cosy seating area and stretching from this is a long old oak refectory table. The curtains are ruched on to pine poles.

At present there is no kitchen but the next stage is to install one next door. This will be an asset for both summer barbeques and winter dinners which at present have to travel the short distance from the main house. Upstairs, the Granary has two beautiful guest bedrooms and a bathroom. The beamed ceilings are high and the windows disproportionately low in relation to the ceiling height so the curtain treatments required some ingenuity.

The garden alongside the Granary was created by local landscape gardener John Hill. He has managed to create, almost instantly, an imaginative flow of different areas incorporating the various buildings and leading them together as one.

VICTORIAN SOLIDITY

This solidly-built Victorian house is situated in a secluded area on the outskirts of Oxford. The sitting room was redecorated two years ago. There was nothing to influence the colour scheme other than the owners' wish that the room should be warm and inviting as it was to be used more in the evening than the day time. The study was the next room to be tackled. The colour scheme is predominantly blues, yellows and golds based around the curtain fabric. All in all, it's a very practical room with an undeniable touch of luxury, just what the owner wanted.

AN ABANDONED FARMHOUSE

My partner Zoë Westropp and her husband, Harry, purchased their current home 10 years ago. The house had not been lived in for some two decades and therefore required total modernization.

The drawing room is a light sunny room with three sides facing the garden and the warmth is enhanced by the yellow colour scheme. It was recently facelifted, for the most part using our own Spencer-Churchill collection fabrics. The walls are painted in a matt eggshell finish also used on the ceiling with the white cornice defining the break between the two.

ABOVE LEFT *The bay window in the Victorian sitting room has become a seating area. The curtain fabric on which the colour scheme is based is a Brook Fairburn paisley design and the wallpaper is a Coles two-tone stripe.*

ABOVE *The study required no major structural work. The bookcases were rebuilt incorporating radiator casings and a dado rail was installed. The walls are covered in a blue flannel fabric above the dado and below they are painted in a stippled finish*

RIGHT *The Westropp's drawing room. The sofa is covered in* Consuelo *from our Blenheim collection and the tablecloth is* Burford, *from the Woodstock collection. Coir matting provides an excellent base for the rug and is also practical.*

The drawing room of this family house is mainly used for entertaining. It is decorated around the Jean Munro chintz used for the curtains. The walls are stippled in a pale champagne colour and the sofa is in a Colefax & Fowler chevron stripe. The Brussels weave carpet has a small blue trellis on a cream background and was made to go with the chintz.

DESIGN FOR A FAMILY

This is a house I spent much time in as a child as it was originally lived in by the Hughes Hallet family whose two sons went to school with my brother James. I can always remember that house having a cosy, lived-in atmosphere, full of life with a mass of people, children and dogs.

When first purchased by its present owners – a young couple – the house had lost that welcoming feeling, and my first reaction on being asked to decorate the house was to reinstate its former warmth and friendliness. Although not a house of great beauty with spectacular architectural features, the rooms were nevertheless well laid out and of good proportions and the house had everything a family could require.

It was decided that the house would be done up gradually, almost room by room, to enable the owners to get a feel for the atmosphere of each room and to give them time to consider the eventual layout of the house. We were also trying to prevent having to re-plan everything the moment that children came along.

ABOVE *An annexe of the same room shown left, which forms another seating area around another fireplace and picks up on the blue theme introduced by the carpet and the cotton dhurrie.*

ABOVE RIGHT *The Cotswold farmhouse dining room was made bigger by removing the chimney. The walls are painted in a blue taken from the Colefax & Fowler chintz. A blue silk sack was made to conceal the chandelier flex, a traditional way to hide such fixings.*

The ground floor is now completed. It is entered either through the front door into a small hallway, or through the back door to the kitchen and utility area. To the left of the hall is a cosy sitting room with an open fireplace, built-in bookcase and television. Down the passage is the drawing room which faces over the garden. It is a bright, sunny room with its own little annexe attached to it which naturally forms a separate seating area.

To the right of the hall is the dining room, a well-proportioned room with windows on two sides. It is primarily used at night and therefore the walls are painted in a cherry-red lacquer drag. The kitchen is a large, practical room with a built-in banquette seat around a table in front of the window. It makes an ideal area for informal eating with the children.

FROM GRAND ESTATE TO FARMHOUSE

The owner of this Cotswold farmhouse had previously owned the magnificent estate and house of Glympton, also in Oxfordshire. The main problem in this case was in moving from a large house to a much smaller one with different proportions while attempting to retain as much furniture and as many of the pictures as possible. Fortunately, the proportions of the new house were generous and not too cottage-like, although, of course, the

ceilings were considerably lower than those of Glympton.

Here we have a very good example of a hall which can be furnished and used as a room. The large stone fireplace (which is not original) provides a wonderful focal point and with a log fire burning, it is an ideal place to congregate for tea after a hard day's hunting or walking. We had to enlarge the hall and add another window to achieve this effect, but the effort was well worthwhile as we succeeded in creating a light, inviting room, in keeping with the owner's expectations.

The dining room leads off the hall and originally had a single door. The double doors were installed in order to make more room to accommodate a magnificent mahogany dining table. The flooring is the original wood plank with rugs on top.

There are two bedrooms housing four-poster beds. In the master bedroom the bed, which came from Glympton, was totally refurbished using the same chintz throughout the room picked out in a blue. Although small in size the room is not overpowered by the four-poster bed – it is a cosy relaxing room. Like the rest of the house it is welcoming and comfortable while retaining elements of grandeur.

COUNTRY PROPERTY

Although situated close to the fast-growing city of Swindon, the backdrop to this house and property is idyllic. Set in a little valley with a stream and lake running through gardens that mix the wild with the formal, you could not be anywhere but the very heart of the English countryside.

Over the last 18 months the property has been undergoing a mammoth refurbishment programme. There are three areas of accommodation: the Stable Block, Garden House and Main House. To enable the owner to have somewhere to stay, the upstairs Stable Block flat was instantly made habitable by installing curtains, carpets and furniture for the three bedrooms, two bathrooms, sitting room and kitchen, and within a few weeks an ideal weekend flat had been put together.

Meanwhile, plans were being drawn up to totally restructure the Garden House. Eventually, this would become the guest house with, perhaps a billiard room included. The existing layout of the Garden House was totally impractical and a complete waste of space. All the bedrooms and bathrooms were replanned, the doors and walls had to be repositioned and the bathrooms are all new. Now finished, the Garden House provides a comfortable, self-sufficient, four-bedroomed house which will become an extremely comfortable guest annexe.

ABOVE LEFT *A guest bathroom that serves two bedrooms. The practical surface is tiled and edged with a wooden frame and a mirror helps to reflect light into this small room. For the present the walls have been left white, waiting for the inevitable shrinkage and cracks that will occur as the plaster dries. Eventually they will be wallpapered.*

ABOVE *A guest bedroom overlooking the garden on the ground floor. It has cream silk curtains for privacy that let in a lovely warm light with a yellowy tinge. The colour scheme is based around the blue and ochre yellow fabric. The floral prints originate from the Victoria and Albert Museum.*

WEEKEND RETREAT

ABOVE *The main bathroom is a little room under the eaves clad in marble and mirror.*

ABOVE RIGHT *The kitchen/dining room. This is the dining end.*

OVERLEAF EMILY'S BEDROOM *Woodstock designs was asked to redecorate a bedroom in a typical 17th century Cotswold manor house. It was for one of the owner's daughters who was reaching her teens and wanted a say in what was chosen. With the sloping beams that run into the ceiling, it made sense to wallpaper both walls and ceiling. We had the original bed copied and covered both in a Colefax & Fowler fabric to match the curtains. The antique lace bedspreads and embroidered cushions add an appropriately feminine touch.*

This typical Cotswold cottage is situated in the middle of a country village. The owner uses it predominantly as a weekend retreat, so our brief was to make it practical, cosy and comfortable yet more than an average cottage. Structurally the house was fairly sound having recently been renovated and a wing added. The previous owners had rented out the property, therefore decoration was required throughout.

The kitchen/dining area was completely gutted and replanned and now the kitchen area, although small, is functional and fitted with hand made units in solid oak styled on the Smallbone unfitted kitchen. The flooring is the original terracotta tiles. The adjacent dining area has a coir matting floor to make it feel separate and more inviting. Tables and chairs are pine and the dresser is a handsome antique painted piece.

Upstairs consists of five bedrooms and two bathrooms. The main bedroom area has its own dressing room with built-in cupboards which leaves the bedroom free for antique pieces of furniture. The main bathroom was totally gutted and replanned and although small, is functional. It is painted in a green simulated wood finish which complements the green of the fabric in the bedroom and gives warmth to what could be a cold room with large expanses of grey marble.

THE OLD APPLE STORE

This Georgian-style country house is situated on an estate in Oxfordshire and was originally the apple store for the main house. The present owner has been there some 25 years over which time he has made various additions to the house and numerous structural alterations.

The entrance hall has the original parquet floor on which lies an antique Persian rug in soft muted tones. The walls have been painted in a bright yellow gloss finish which reflects the light and is a good background colour for furniture and pictures.

To the left of the hall is the new wing which comprises a guest bedroom and bathroom and conservatory on the ground floor and master bedroom and bathroom above.

The master bedroom is decorated in a blue *toile de jouy* fabric and the en-suite bathroom has a spacious country feel. The bath and basin have mahogany panels and vanitory units which, along with the free-standing pieces of furniture, give warmth and character to the room. The walls are papered in a Sanderson paper

above the dado and the curtains and chair seat are in a Colefax & Fowler printed cotton. The antique engravings in gilt frames add to the character of the room.

The opposite wing of the house consists of library and drawing room on the ground floor and guest bedrooms above. The drawing room is decorated in soft muted pinks, beiges and blues. The curtain fabric is a Colefax & Fowler chintz with a swags and tails pelmet edged with a frill and lined in a plain pink chintz.

The walls are in a strawberry pink drag paint finish and the rest of the furnishings are in neutral colours. The antique chair has a wonderful faded hand-embroidered tapestry cover with antique brass studs. The candelabra is antique and lit by candles.

There is no formal dining room in the house and the dining area is an extension of the kitchen built as a conservatory. It is treated very much as a country garden room with plants all around the room and French country furniture. The floor is imitation flagstones with a modern dhurrie rug set on top to break up the expanse of stone floor. At night there are no blinds to let down but the garden is floodlit which gives atmosphere to the room, making the guests feel they are in the garden.

The main guest bedroom upstairs has a brass partly-painted bed. The walls have been papered in a Spencer-Churchill Designs *Woodstock* wallpaper and a Coles wallpaper border instead of a cornice. The curtains and roller blind are in Spencer-Churchill Designs *Balmoral*.

ABOVE LEFT *The corner cupboards in the drawing room came originally from Syrie Maugham, the famous interior designer of the 1930s and wife of the writer Somerset Maugham. They have been restored and wired for lighting.*

ABOVE *The scheme for the main guest bedroom is based around the antique bedspread.*

RIGHT *The en-suite bathroom belonging to the master bedroom has a lovely old fashioned air.*

PREVIOUS PAGE LEFT *In the bright yellow entrance hall is a portrait by Lavery of Lady Furness, mother of the present owner, Lord Waterpark.*

PREVIOUS PAGE RIGHT *The dining room is in a conservatory extension. At night there are no blinds to let down, but the garden is floodlit.*

A COTSWOLD COTTAGE

This Cotswold stone cottage dates from 1640. It has retained many of its original features and, unlike many cottages, has not been spoilt by crude later additions. It is the home of Ian Walton who is the main design consultant on our decorating side. Ian divides his time between Oxfordshire and London where he has a duplex. He moved in here about four years ago and, fortunately, the cottage required little structural alteration. The rooms are small and ceilings low, so it was a question of making the best use of the space available without allowing it to become overcrowded and cluttered.

The entrance is really nothing more than a lobby with three doors opening off it, so there is no room for any furniture, and only just enough space for the umbrella stand. In order to create a warm welcome, the walls were painted in a soft yellow to look like mock stone. The right-hand door leads into the dining room and the left into the sitting room. On the floor are the original flagstones, typical of country cottages and farmhouses and luckily, in this case, they were in very good condition.

The dining room doubles up as a library. With many hundreds of books to house it was necessary to build bookshelves wherever possible. Virtually every window in the cottage is of a different shape and size and at varying levels which made window treatments awkward. Each window needed to be treated as an individual, but at the same time they had to relate to one another. As there was no cornice in the room, the pelmets were taken to the ceiling in order to let in as much light as possible. The fabric used is a Pallu & Lake design called *Mikado*, edged in a plain chintz.

The walls are painted in a flat John Oliver paint finish, called *Refford Red*, the colour taken from the curtains. Around the cornice line is a Cole & Son paper border which acts as a cornice and forms a break between ceiling and walls. During the day the refectory table is used without a cloth and in the evening a blue/grey tablecloth is used. The Edwardian credenza under the window is used as a drinks tray and the grandfather clock is 18th century. The owner of the house collects antique microscopes and telescopes hence the array of instruments and related objects scattered around the rooms.

The sitting room is a small cosy place in which a roaring fire burns virtually all year round. The ceiling is low and so the

beams were painted rather than stained in order to heighten the ceiling visually. The walls are painted in a flat emulsion paint in a dark mustard colour taken from the crewel fabric which I had purchased in India a few years ago.

The room has five windows, all of different sizes. On the large window the curtains hang from a wooden pole on rings and the four smaller windows have inset Roman blinds, chosen because they are both simple and neat. The woodwork was dragged in a lighter version of the walls and the floorcovering is sisal – an ideal base for rugs. There are no overhead lights and wall lights have been used instead of table lamps as they would have taken up too much valuable space.

A small turning staircase with bare oak treads and handrails leads to the upstairs. The walls of the stairwell are in fake block-work, like the hallway below. The colours in the main bedroom are very light and bright, the walls are off-white to complement the freestanding mahogany furniture and the floral chintz used for the curtains is a GP & J Baker design in cheerful yellows and blues. The small, carpeted bathroom has a floral wallpaper to give it depth and the original bath together with its old-fashioned pillar taps which were rescued from the old downstairs wash-house and lovingly restored.

The cottage exudes a lot of style. It is very much a designer version of the classic English look with enormous attention paid to every last detail – essential when space is at a premium.

ABOVE LEFT *The charming entrance hall of this tiny cottage is no bigger than a cupboard. The walls are painted in a stone effect finish, the floor is of old flagstones.*

ABOVE *The dining room doubles up as a study cum library during the day.*

RIGHT *Detail of a window in the dining room surrounded by yet more bookcases.*

PREVIOUS PAGE *In the sitting room not an inch of space is wasted.*

MANOR HOUSE WITH VICTORIAN ADDITIONS

Situated in the heart of Oxfordshire, this is another house in which I spent much time as a child. The previous owner had a daughter of my age and we were at the same nursery school in a nearby village. The present owners have been here for some years and have made many improvements to the house.

The front door leads into an outer hall and then into the main hall off which run the drawing room, library and main staircase. The hall has linenfold oak panelling three quarters of the way up the wall and above this, plasterwork panels depict various shields.

The library leads off the hall up some steps and is therefore on a higher level. There is a small landing leading into the main area which houses a desk under the window – a sensible use of an otherwise wasted space. The fireplace is located on an angled wall opposite the window shown in the photograph. Deciding on a layout for the furniture was not easy as it was impossible to group

LEFT *Arabella, the eldest daughter, inherited her grandmother's four-poster bed which has been restored and re-covered using a Colefax & Fowler chintz and a Warner's fancy lining for the sunburst ceiling.*

RIGHT *The second daughter's bedroom now houses two single beds. The chintz is by Colefax & Fowler and the soft furnishings have been picked out in a plain pink chintz. The painting over the dressing table is by Seago, one of my favourite artists.*

PREVIOUS PAGE *The large open fireplace in the hall is a mixture of stone and wood, the top part carved from an original 17th century beam, the lower half of carved stone. It now houses a wood burning stove which gives off enough heat to filter up the staircase. The room is simply furnished in reds and naturals and it is generally used as a place to relax and read the Sunday papers or have tea or drinks after a day's shooting.*

PAGE 118 *The core of this manor house dates from the 17th century, but most of the existing structure is Victorian. From the outside, with its stone mullion windows, it looks as if it could be dark and gloomy, but inside it is surprisingly light and airy.*

PAGE 119 *The library is the everyday sitting room, used to watch television and entertain small numbers of guests. The curtains are in a wonderful heavy red wool edged in braid and the Colefax & Fowler Hollyhock chintz brings in a breath of colour and light.*

pieces around the fireplace. During the day, while the curtains in front of the window seat are drawn back, the window seats provide additional seating but when the curtains are drawn, this is lost.

With the owners' three children now grown up, the two daughters' bedrooms were recently redecorated to their own requirements. In the bedroom of the elder daughter, Arabella, the walls are papered in Cole & Son wallpaper in an old-fashioned soft pink. There is a fabric-covered dressing table set into the bow window and the whole room gives off an air of total comfort and invites you to flop into the comfortable bed.

What is now the second daughter's bedroom I can remember being the old nursery and it was always a friendly living room. It now houses two single beds and still retains the fireplace. Originally, there were built-in cupboards either side of the fireplace but these were removed to give a feeling of more space. The Portuguese white cotton bedspreads give an air of freshness to the room and set off the brass bedheads.

This house reflects the typical English country house style – relaxed yet elegant, formal but friendly.

The L-shaped drawing room on the first floor takes its decorative theme from the curtain fabric, a Titley & Marr chintz. The curtains are edged in a plain blue and the pelmets have swags and tails and a jabot in the centre. The walls are painted in a pinky lilac to go with the marble fireplace. On the beige carpet are several antique Persian rugs.

RIGHT *The study has a conservatory leading off it to provide extra seating. It is a warm, cosy room used mainly at night. The television is hidden under the red velvet tablecloth.*

KNIGHTSBRIDGE TOWN HOUSE

This London house is situated on one of London's most attractive crescents. It has five floors and although tall, it is wider than the average town house so the rooms have very elegant proportions. To provide additional space, two conservatories were added. The one in the basement is an addition to the kitchen, forming an eating area on one side and a small playroom on the other. The second was added on the ground floor as an extension to the study providing an extra seating or reading area.

The study, an everything room housing the television, had bookcases installed and a new fire surround. The walls and woodwork were painted in a *faux bois* green to give a dark intimate feel. The colour scheme is red and green taken from the curtain fabric, a popular Percheron chintz.

The first floor consists of one large L-shaped drawing room with three large windows. This is a formal room used mainly in the evening for entertaining. Because of its size we could create different seating areas without dividing the room up too much.

The main bedroom and bathroom are on the second floor. The existing cupboards were badly planned so new ones were built in both rooms. The bedroom units were designed for women's clothes and the bathroom cupboards for men's. On the next floor up there is a bathroom on the half landing and three more bedrooms. The two children's bedrooms are to the front and have a double door connecting them. At night, this is closed but during the day it is left open to provide a communal play area.

This large, comfortable home works well for formal entertaining as well as for relaxed family life.

VICTORIAN DUPLEX

This London duplex belongs to Ian Walton, Woodstock's consultant designer. From here he entertains on a lavish scale and with great ease. The sitting room and dining room are connected but divided by double-sided curtains. During the day, the dining area has a relaxed, informal country feel to it with views over the garden, an old pine kitchen table and long benches either side. At night, for entertaining, the room is dressed up. A white damask tablecloth covers the homely pine table and soft lighting changes the whole atmosphere.

The walls in both rooms are wallpapered in a Zoffany marbled wallpaper in a warm salmon colour taken from the Ramm,

ABOVE LEFT *Small guest bedroom on a half landing is all built in. Even the lights are wall-mounted to save space.*

ABOVE *In the conservatory off the study, Roman blinds in rattan shade the windows and wicker furniture provides seating.*

RIGHT *The dining room of Ian Walton's duplex is divided from the sitting room by a double-sided curtain. The fireplace is a focal point rather than a working fire, radiators are cased in either side of it. There are no overhead lights, all the lighting comes from picture lights and candles.*

OVERLEAF LEFT *The sitting room is dominated by the dramatic curtain treatment.*

OVERLEAF RIGHT *A view of the sitting room showing the lovely mahogany day bed and the upholstered stool.*

Son & Crocker chintz. The floors are wooden plank with rugs thrown on top to break up and define areas. Part of the cornice is picked out in a dark green emphasizing the coved area.

The seating area of the sitting room is laid out to provide as much seating as possible and the William IV mahogany day bed comfortably holds three people providing an attractive alternative to the conventional upholstered sofa. Ian purchased the ends of the day bed in an antique shop and had the centre struts made up to match. It is a lovely period piece.

The buttoned ottoman acts as a coffee table as well as a stool, it has a firm enough surface to take a trayful of drinks without wobbling. The lighting is a mixture of lamps, picture lights and downlighters on a dimmer switch. The alabaster lamp in the bay window is a converted vase. The engravings over the day bed were purchased as a set in a junk shop. Now restored and framed, they provide an ideal decorative wall feature.

Downstairs is another open plan sitting room where the television and desk are located, leaving the upstairs room more formal for entertaining. The bedroom and bathroom are also in the basement. It is a small but stylish home.

ABOVE *The bathroom in Ian Walton's London home is functional, incorporating a shower in the bath which operates independently from the taps and at the other end of the bath so you do not have to lean in awkwardly. The towel rail is mounted on the wall above the bath so you can wrap yourself in a warm towel before you step dripping wet onto the carpet. The walls are papered in a Jane Churchill wallpaper and the festoon curtain is in a Pallu & Lake* Glenalmond *fabric edged with a plain chintz, the same colour as the tiles. The basin unit was built especially high to incorporate the sill. Chrome fittings have been used throughout.*

RIGHT A TYPICAL LONDON TOWN HOUSE. *The sitting room has a very high ceiling and a large window and so it was able to take a nice deep pelmet edged with a fringe. The colour scheme has been taken from the chintz and the walls were painted with a hint of pink as white would have been too stark. The round table by the window hides a television and the square coffee table is painted with a green lacquer finish.*

OVERLEAF A BEAUTIFUL DRAWING ROOM. *The magnificent Italian mirror over the mantlepiece is the focal point of this green and cream room and the green is cleverly picked up in the mounts of the prints on the left as well as on the elaborately painted cornice.*

MEWS COTTAGE

This tiny mews house in the centre of London is the perfect home for a single girl. It is easy to maintain and exudes warmth and friendliness. It was decided that the sitting room and hall should remain open plan rather than creating an entrance lobby which would have broken into the already small sitting room. The study area was made slightly separate by leaving part of the partition wall in place. The built-in bookshelves were designed and custom built to provide a focal point.

Upstairs consists of two small bedrooms. The master bedroom has a shower en suite and the second bedroom has a bathroom opposite. The smaller bedroom is used more as a dressing room, and built-in cupboards were installed here to allow more space in the main bedroom. It is a tiny house but it doesn't feel in the least claustrophobic because all the furniture has been scaled down in size to suit the miniscule dimensions.

ABOVE *The tiny sitting room and the hall are open plan so you walk into the sitting room directly from the front door. The colour scheme is based on reds and the Brussels weave carpet was specially commissioned.*

RIGHT *The kitchen was not large enough to have an eating area so a small round glass and perspex table was placed by the French doors. The idea was to apply for planning permission at a later stage to build a conservatory into the garden to provide an eating area, and this has since been acquired.*

BELGRAVIA TERRACE

This was a large family house and our brief was to gut it totally and remodernize it for a bachelor. It had been lived in by a family for some time and although perfectly habitable, had not undergone any recent modernization in the way of plumbing, wiring or general maintenance. It was one of those typical houses where on the surface things do not look too bad but when you start ripping things out, unsuspected defects are discovered. This was certainly the case here and as the initial contract progressed it became obvious that there were areas outside our brief such as leaking roofs and parapets and rotten floor joists which simply could not be ignored.

Despite its size, the house lacked a dining room and therefore we decided to apply for planning permission to add on a garden room between the basement and ground floor. Fortunately, consent was speedily given and with the help of architect Charles Knowles the construction commenced using the same builders who were carrying out works in the rest of the house.

The whole project took almost a year. Every room was completely rewired and replumbed. A piped stereo system and a comprehensive security and television sysem were also installed – I have never seen so many cables running from room to room.

On the top floor, the layout was changed to provide two

ABOVE LEFT *The main bathroom had to be totally stripped and laid out from scratch. The bath was positioned so that you can see out of the window while lying in the bath. The mural reflected in the large mirror is painted on board.*

ABOVE *The main bedroom faces onto the street and, as there is a dressing room nearby, the room is unencumbered with cupboards and chests of drawers so it is as elegant as a country house bedroom with lovely pieces of freestanding antique furniture. The chintz curtain fabric is by Ramm, Son & Crocker and the wallpaper is a Coles two-tone stripe.*

RIGHT *The drawing room on the ground floor is an L-shaped room with a colour scheme of greens and yellows.*

Two views of the new dining room, built out from the ground floor as a conservatory. Only part of the roof is glazed to ensure privacy from a nearby block of flats. The windows have been left without curtains or blinds as the room is not overlooked and it is used mainly at night when glare from the sun is not a problem. The table was specially designed for the room. It is a pedestal table painted in a marbleized finish that can be extended to seat 12 people. The French cane chairs are painted to match the table. It is very much custom-designed down to the Italianate murals and the slate floor.

bedrooms and a separate bathroom. The floor below has a double bedroom and bathroom en suite and a large room, presently used as a study, with its own sink and fridge concealed in a cupboard. The floor below is the master suite with bedroom, dressing room and bathroom all en suite. There is also separate access into the dressing room from the landing. The bedroom is such a well-proportioned space it would have been ruined with built-in cupboards, so it is furnished with free-standing pieces and a marble fireplace. The built-in cupboards in the dressing room were custom-designed with a hardwood finish inside. There is a day bed, either to be used as a sofa for watching television or as an extra guest bed. The bathroom, which is light and airy, leads off the dressing room and was completely refitted including demolishing a lowered ceiling which cut off part of the window.

The ground floor drawing room consists of two rooms leading into one another providing two definite seating areas. The back area leading to the garden originally contained a chimney breast which extended right throughout the building. We removed this to give additional space in all the back rooms. The colour scheme was taken from a fabric designed by Simon Playle. The brief was

The study upstairs was originally two rooms with an awkward lobby in between. The fabric on the walls is a cotton ticking which goes well with the coral and grey printed curtain fabric.

for a simple, smart room without too much fussy detail which would show off his fine antiques and paintings.

Leading to the new garden room was an existing small ante-room which now provides either an additional eating area or an area from which to service the main room. Rather than ruin the walls of the new garden room with radiators, and I dislike skirting radiators, we decided to install underfloor heating with a grill running around the perimeter of the room. It was not only a practical solution but also effective in design terms.

The kitchen, located in the basement, was always dark and dingy. In order to let in additional light we installed a French door and a full length window to the small patio outside. This not only provides extra light but also a view from the eating area in the kitchen. The kitchen units, yellow-painted wood finish, were made and installed by a country firm and we chose the colour to brighten the place up. Also located in the basement is a self-contained flat, ideal for a resident housekeeper.

The house works well now for a bachelor but it could easily be altered to accommodate a family, without any further expensive and time-consuming structural alterations.

AT HOME

ABOVE *The dining end of my kitchen showing the wallpaper and the check fabric that give the room a warm, country feeling. The pictures are by Arthur Bryne who specializes in architectural garden scenes.*

ABOVE RIGHT *My bedroom on the top floor is a light and sunny room but it is hot in summer and extremely cold in the winter. My dressing table and stool were already covered in a Simon Playle fabric* Scène Chinoise *which I loved so I decided to use it to finish off the room. The walls were yellow, a colour I wouldn't have chosen, but I decided to keep as it gave the room a cheerful feeling. The watercolour over the bed was painted by my grandmother, Nicole Hornby.*

Whilst house hunting for a suitable house for myself and two children the main requirement was to find something that I could move into instantly. I did not have the time or energy to cope with a massive refurbishment programme, especially after dealing with everyone else's decorating dilemmas day in, day out.

After looking at about 30 properties within the space of a few days I instantly settled for this one which had just been refurbished by a small developer following a recent fire in the house. The layout was ideal for my needs with the rooms located on three floors and a small garden leading off the kitchen.

Knowing that the house was only to be a stepping stone for a couple of years I did not want to spend a lot of time and money on the decoration. I had existing furniture, most of which fitted ideally into the various rooms. Initially, I hung plain white or cream roller blinds in all of the rooms to give privacy while I contemplated whether or not to have curtains.

The kitchen was already fitted with a range of pine units so it seemed logical to carry on the country feel. I bought a pine table and bench for the eating area and four single chairs which comfortably seat six to eight people. If I want to seat more people then I have another folding table which I put up in the conservatory area where I can seat another six.

141

Two views of my sitting room which was a case of making the best out of what was there without changing too much. The wallpaper was neutral and inoffensive as was the carpet. The two coral armchairs in the window are covered in a patterned velvet. The one with castors is the original, the other is a copy made by an upholsterer in Oxfordshire.

The walls were originally painted in a stone colour which was slightly cold and uninviting so I recently added the Interior Selection wallpaper with terracotta and bluey-green flowers which adds warmth to the room and ties in well with the terracotta tiled floor. The blind and cushion covers are in a Turnell & Gigon check which is also on the bench seat, but protected with a towelling cover to counteract the effects of dogs and children

The sitting room has not been touched and I have left the two-tone stripe wallpaper as I felt it provided a good background for my collection of watercolours. Purchased over a number of years, I have picked them up from various junk shops and had them all renovated and framed. The carpet is a twist pile and, although not one I would have selected, it again made a good base for rugs. The curtains, which are purely dress curtains and do not draw are in a Colefax & Fowler chintz which tied in well with my existing furnishings.

On the floor above, there are three bedrooms and a bathroom where the children and nanny sleep. Further upstairs again is another room, which I use as a study, and my bedroom and en-suite bathroom which is a loft conversion.

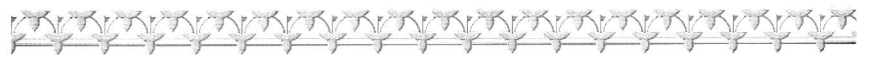

PART TWO

THE LEXICON

COLOUR AND PATTERN

More than any other single factor, colour establishes the character of a room. It is no easy task to establish that character and pick a colour scheme that you will be happy to live with, year in year out, that will complement your chosen style of furniture and provide a suitable backdrop for your treasured possessions. Courage is what you need when choosing a colour scheme, courage and experience, and although you can always buy the experience of a reliable interior decorator, the courage has to come from within.

COLOUR AND LIGHT

Light, both natural and artificial, is the key element in judging any proposed colour scheme, as colours and tones change depending on the degree and type of light they are subjected to, be it direct sunlight, dull grey daylight, a low voltage glow or the piercing beam of a spotlight. It is important therefore to study your proposed colours in varying degrees of light in the room in which they will eventually be used and to ascertain whether that room is to be used principally by day or by night.

COLOUR AND MOOD

Different colours will produce varying degrees of warmth and coolness. These will again be affected by texture and finish regardless of the fact that the colours appear

THE BLUES

Inset *Wallpaper and roller blind in* SCD Windrush, *curtains in* Folly *by Putnams with a smart plain blue chintz backing.*
1 *A kitchen scheme, l to r: plain blue chintz for edging;* SCD wallpaper, Bladon; *C&F check linen for seat*

3

5

4

6

cushions; *SCD fabric* Wychwood *for curtains and blue stipple tiles.*
2 *Kitchen corner in SCD fabric* Glympton *and matching wallpaper.*
3 *The 5th Duchess's watercolour that inspired the fabric,* Rosamund.
4 *Bedroom scheme, l to r: damask for bedspread by Harris Fabrics,*

Wallpaper by Caroline Ward, Jab Blue Ribbon *chintz and SCD* Rosamund *for curtains. In the foreground a self-patterned O&L upholstery fabric,* Dobbyweave.
5 *Dining room scheme, clockwise from l: blue velvet for dress curtains held in place by tassel tie-backs with wooden*

ends; Warner's printed chintz for festoon curtains, fringed in blue; damask fabric by Pierre Frey.
6 *Bathroom curtains and box-pleated pelmet in C&F two-tone* Paris *to match the upholstered seat back, teamed with a bright green roller blind. The wallpaper is* Sonnet *by Sanderson.*

to be the same; because reflective surfaces, like tiles, will throw off different tones from those that absorb light, like carpets. A surprising amount of variety can be achieved in a monochrome scheme by juxtaposing different textures and finishes.

Most people are aware that blues are cold and reds are warm, but they often overlook the fact that this rule applies to furniture and pictures as much as it does to walls. A maroon velvet sofa with a sumptuous fringe would look as out of place in a bright, light room as a stark white armchair would in the midst of dark Victorian clutter.

COLOUR LINK

Planning a colour scheme for a whole house at once is a daunting task. The temptation is either to opt for safety and paint everything white or to use a riot of different colours in every room. Both these solutions can be very effective if handled with care.

What is required of any colour scheme is a link, a sense of continuity between rooms so that the eye will travel smoothly and not jump from one colour to another. This is easy enough to achieve if all the walls in the house have been painted in a neutral colour with each individual room asserting its own personality with strong printed fabrics, patterned rugs or beautiful pictures. If you want different colours in each room, then a link can be established by using colours of the same tonal value, or by linking the furniture styles or the carpet colour.

Passages and stairways and open plan areas are key linking spaces. These can either be treated as one to allow your eye to travel smoothly along them or they can be made to change, gradually and subtly, to allow your eyes to adapt to the surprises in store in the next room.

PERSONAL CHOICE

Colour choices are very personal. In decorating terms it is as well to try and relate colour to its purpose. A certain shade of blue may look wonderful made up as a skirt or on a piece of porcelain, but that does not mean

1

2

3

6

5

7

YELLOWS AND GREENS
1 *Garden room scheme, l to r: patterned and striped linens from Dovedale; rattan blinds and seagrass matting.*
2 *Kitchen table with painted marble-effect top and stained wood frame.*
3 *Drawing room scheme, clockwise from l: C&F* Paris *fabric for the blinds;*

SCD Mey *for the dress curtains; plain green moiré from Textiles FCD for upholstery; needlepoint rug from Afia.*
4 *A fresh, sunny London drawing room with chintz curtains and a sofa in a Percheron striped cotton.*
5 *Decorative paintwork and inlay work on a console table.*

6 *A bedroom and en-suite bathroom scheme, clockwise from l: C&F wallpaper and complementary border; C&F wool fabric for bedspread and upholstery; curtain chintz from Warners; carpet from Afia.*
7 *One of the 5th Duchess's evocative watercolours.*

to say that it will work as well plastered over four walls. Any one colour used on its own will dominate a room, and if it is a strong colour it may absorb other colours and even distract the eye from the proportions of the room.

THE STARTING POINT

More often than not, the choice of colour and design will be governed by existing features – wallpaper, a pair of curtains, a carpet or an accessory such as a painting, a rug or a collection of porcelain.

If this is the case, then you should decide whether you wish that piece to dominate the room or to blend into the overall scheme. If it is to dominate, then the rest of the room treatment should be subdued, using soft, harmonizing colours. If it is to blend in, then you can lessen the impact by repeating one or more of its colours in similar intensity elsewhere in the room.

If, for example, you are stuck with a carpet or curtains that you do not particularly like but cannot afford to change immediately, then careful choice of other fabrics, both patterned and plain, will certainly help to distract the eye and focus attention in other directions.

Architectural features can play a part in the selection and treatment of colour. For example a panelled wall or an exotic, decorative ceiling may call for special treatment, or the period of the house may inspire you to base your scheme upon an authentic colour associated with that particular style – a blue-tinged Williamsburg green, for example, an art-deco peach or a neo-classical Wedgwood blue.

A good balance of colour, texture and pattern is difficult to achieve. There are no hard and fast rules about using colours together, it is very much dependent on personal taste and on the individual eye. Once you have established the basic colours you want to work with, experiment with different tones and textures within your chosen spectrum, as you will find that some work better together than others.

THE REDS

1 *Scheme for a drawing room, from l: walls in* Murasuede; *Marvic's* Misa *striped upholstery fabric for the sofa; paisley curtain fabric from J. Brooke Fairburn and a length of printed velvet for the cushions.*
2 *Bedroom scheme, clockwise from l:*

150

3

5

4

6

*wallpaper and border by Nina
Campbell; stripe fabric for the curtains
by O&L with tie-backs and fringes
from Henry Newberry; trellis-
patterned wool upholstery fabric Sulley
by Marvic; fabric for blinds and bed
valances Asthis leaf design by SCD.*
3 *Pretty upholstered armchair in a rose-*

pink cut velvet with a rope trim.
4 *'Pelargonium Tricolour' painted by
the 5th Duchess in October 1795.*
5 *Scheme for a study, clockwise from l:
wool tartan from Isle Mill Ltd for
upholstering the sofa and fringe to trim
it; linen fabric for the walls; a
Dovedale leaf design chintz for the*

curtains and tapestry for a wing chair.
6 *Red felt walls and full-length fringed
curtains give this room a rich,
welcoming feeling.*

A DIFFERENT EMPHASIS

The same colour scheme will assume a quite different character if the proportions of the colours are changed. This can be used to good effect, not only from one room to the next but also within a large room that you wish to divide visually into distinct areas.

For instance, you might decide to use one end of a large drawing room as a dining area. You could give the dining end a more intimate character by picking out one of the darker, richer, accent colours from the over-all scheme and using it in an upholstery fabric for the dining chairs or on a well-positioned screen or rug.

PATTERNS

Different combinations of colour, texture and pattern can either be stunning or disastrous. Patterns are not easily ignored, they have a tremendous impact on a room and they must be selected with a great deal of care and attention.

Before making any decisions, analyze the room and work out exactly which pattern fabric or wallpaper is to be used where and gather together samples of everything you intend to use in the room including carpets, rugs, paints and cushion covers to ensure that they will work together harmoniously. Consider the scale of the pattern in relation to the scale of the room and where it is being used. There is no point using a large scale design on a tiny window and a tiny design in a huge room will just get lost.

Another consideration is the type of fabric or paper, because the same pattern can look very different printed on an unglazed cotton or woven into a heavy linen, just as a machine-printed wallpaper looks different from handmade paper that has been silk-screened. Remember too, that a pattern incorporating many different colours and details will look far richer than a design using just two or three.

Patterns do go with patterns, and many successful looks have been put together piling pattern upon pattern. Obviously, there must be some sort of relationship between

1

2

WHITE ON WHITE

1 *A studio scheme, clockwise from l: bedroom curtains in SCD* Consuelo *chintz with rope wool tiebacks; sitting area curtains in an Indian crewel fabric from Coromandel; white silk bedhangings from Sussex Silks; self-patterned* Piedmont *fabric by Marvic*

5

6

3

4

for the bedspread.
2 *Dressing room scheme, from l: cotton moiré on the walls; Ian Sanderson* Candance *stripe for the bed valance; grey and white* toile de Jouy *for the curtains and a self-patterned fabric for the bedspread from Nobilis Fontan.*
3 *Shades of white and cream in the bathroom enlivened by a simulated marble bath alcove and a floral screen to hide the towel rail.*
4 *The master bedroom that goes with the bathroom shown above. The only non-white element is the chintz used for the blind and for lining the bedcurtains.*
5 *Drawing room scheme, from l: wallpaper is by Zoffany, as is the paper border; Gainsborough white damask for the curtains; the chevron stripe upholstery fabric is by C&F, the carpet a Brussels loop design from Newgate Carpets.*
6 *Lily of the valley by the 5th Duchess.*

the patterns and some other element in the room that ties everything together. Many fabric and wallpaper collections are designed to mix and match, but if you want to go it alone, start by looking at patterns using the same colours and design but to a different scale, or find patterns that use the same range of colours but with a completely different emphasis.

WALLPAPERS

Select the colour and pattern of your wallpaper bearing in mind the other textures in the room, and choose the scale of the pattern in relation to the size of the room. A striped wallpaper in a room with low ceilings will help make the walls appear taller, a plain, pale design will help make the room feel considerably larger.

Wallpaper borders are now widely available and will often co-ordinate with the wallpaper or a fabric from the same collection. They look effective finishing off the top of the wall, especially if there is no cornice in the room, or they can be used to form panels or to highlight certain features such as doors or windows.

COLOUR AND SPACE

The inter-relationship of colour and light has an effect on the visual (as opposed to actual) size and shape of the room – even of the whole house or apartment. Neutral colours are space enhancing, and give a peaceful, classical feel to a room. Dark, sombre colours create a warm, intimate feeling and give the illusion of bringing the walls closer in, making the room seem smaller.

Using this knowledge you can visually alter the proportions of rooms. For instance, an old house that has been converted into flats may contain some small rooms with disproportionately high ceilings. In such a case, the use of a darker colour on the ceiling will visually lower it and make the room seem better proportioned. In a room with a low ceiling, the use of the same light colour on walls, floor and ceiling will make the room seem larger and lighter.

1

2

THE PALE SPECTRUM

1 *Drawing room scheme, clockwise from l: for the sofa, a linen upholstery fabric from Bennison,* Monochrome roses; *for the walls,* Shagreen *from O&L; for the curtains a* toile de Jouy *by Marvic and for accent a fabric by Lorenzo Rubelli.*

3

5

4

6

2 *Scheme for a breakfast room in a selection of mix and match SCD* Windrush *and* Evenlode *fabrics and wallpapers. The upholstery fabric is* Tavistock *by C&F.*

3 *An elegantly pale corner of a bedroom that successfully marries beiges, yellows and creams.*

4 *A charming watercolour by Susan Blandford, 5th Duchess of Marlborough. It was her watercolours that inspired a range of Spencer-Churchill Designs fabrics.*

5 *Design for a bedroom, clockwise from l: wallpaper and matching border are by Hill & Knowles; SCD* Leaves *chintz*

for the curtains; a Busby & Busby striped chintz for the blinds, a wonderful woven fabric from Textiles FCD for the bedspread and peach linen for the upholstery.

6 *A pale and pretty guest bedroom with traditional chintz and smart windowpane checks.*

Contrasting colours can be used to accentuate beautiful plasterwork or panelling. Alternatively, if the room has architectural features that are less than attractive, they can be made inconspicuous by painting them to blend in using the same colour as the surrounding elements.

FABRICS

Depending on the way it is treated, a fabric can assume a range of different looks. For instance a floral chintz containing many colours could make a wonderful pair of bedroom curtains when gathered and pleated and edged with pink while the same fabric can take on a different personality as a neatly tailored chair cover, piped with a dark green. Equally the use of different coloured paints or wallpapers can alter the effect of a multicoloured fabric by highlighting one particular aspect of the colourway.

Choosing a patterned fabric from the vast choice available is very much a question of personal taste and, while obviously colour and pattern are of prime importance, consideration must also be given to the suitability of the fabric for its intended purpose. Do ask for advice, if necessary from the manufacturer, on the durability and the washability of the fabrics you have chosen and remember that lengthy exposure to direct sunlight will cause most fabrics to fade.

A QUESTION OF BALANCE

When the paint and paper and fabrics are finally all in place, you may find that you have not got the balance quite right – that the room lacks coherence and is too 'busy' or, conversely, that it is too bland. Such problems can be corrected in various ways, by a careful choice of accessories – it's amazing what an armful of colourful cushions and a couple of healthy houseplants can do – or an adjustment of the lighting.

The best advice, however, is to think carefully about colour before you buy anything. The more you live with colour the more you will understand it and learn to use it with assurance and flair.

THE DARK SPECTRUM

1 *Scheme for a study, clockwise from l: wallpaper from Zoffany; woollen upholstery tartan from Isle Mill Ltd; Warners chintz with a burgundy-coloured ground for the curtains with tie-backs and fringes from Henry Newberry; blue-green upholstery fabric*

3

5

4

6

from Sanderson and a woven fabric for the sofa from Manuel Canovas.

2 *Dark and dramatic: drawing room curtains in a Titley and Marr chintz teamed with a sofa in a bold striped satin that picks up colours from the antique Persian rug.*

3 *Corner of a sitting room in different*

tones and textures of green. The walls are in a rag-rolled wallpaper from M. Short, the bookcase in a simulated wood lacquered finish, the wing chair is upholstered in an ottoman fabric and the lampshade is of pleated silk.

4 *Scheme for a library, clockwise from l: Pallu & Lake curtain fabric with co-*

ordinating small design for blinds; the fabric on the walls is Renishaw from Marvic and the patterned linen fabric for the sofa is from Stothert and Miles.

5 *Striking colours in a watercolour by Susan Blandford, circa 1795.*

6 *A hand-painted dresser with stencilled panels, circa 1980.*

WALLS

Classical architects divided the wall into two distinct parts with three horizontal bands: the cornice, which provides a natural break between wall and ceiling; the dado rail, which is the height of a chair back and was originally intended to protect walls from scuffing, and the skirting rail, which neatens the join between floor and wall. If you live in an old house, you may be lucky enough to be left with some of these original features, which certainly do serve to enhance proportions. If they have been ripped out, they can easily be replaced and if your home is newly built and your walls are blank you may find the addition of a few simple mouldings will give the place some character.

CORNICES AND SKIRTINGS

Cornices can be as plain or as elaborate as you like. They certainly help to finish off a room and provide a natural break between the wall treatment and the ceiling. Dado rails will help to break up a large expanse of wall. Walls are often treated differently above the dado rail and below it. Skirtings are essential to finish off the wall and prevent walls from being damaged. They should be made of hardwood and their depth should be in proportion to the height of the ceiling.

Other architectural wall-enhancing features include picture rails, panel mouldings, pillars, ceiling roses and architraves, all of

PAINT EFFECTS
Inset *Cleverly faked interpretation of old Cotswold stone.*
1 *A period 18th-century door painted in a drag effect to match the walls in order to lessen its visual impact. The delicate mouldings on both door and walls are highlighted in gilt.*

3

5

4

6

2 *Panelled door painted in three different tones to highlight the panels. Generally the main part of the door is painted in the darker colour and the panels in a lighter shade. Here the two-tone panel has a light surround and a medium shade in the centre. Beadings have been left white for contrast.*

3 *A bright, warm yellow has been used between cornice and dado rail, and the woodwork is smartly painted in a contrasting gloss white.*

4 *A combed and dragged paint finish gives a simulated wood effect.*

5 *An example of a beautifully carved moulding, highlighted in white against*

a darker ground.

6 *Subtly dragged door. A slightly darker shade has been used on the main part of the door, a little more white has been added to the panels to make them stand out and the beading around the edge of the panels is wiped with a hint of green.*

which can be bought off the shelf in a variety of classical and modern designs or even custom-made.

PLASTER

Generally speaking, walls are plastered or plasterboarded to obtain a smooth, even finish, but a rough plaster effect can look good in the appropriate setting. When dealing with an old house, beware of making the walls look too even or new. A few lumps and bumps and uneven corners will give the house back some of its original character.

BRICK AND STONE

Exposed brick or stonework works well if used in moderation – for instance around a fireplace or in a kitchen surrounding an old stove – but it must be sealed or painted to cut out dust and draughts.

WOOD PANELLING

Expensive but practical, wood panelling acts as an insulator and will improve acoustics. The cheapest type of panelling is tongue and groove, which can be used horizontally, vertically or diagonally. It is particularly attractive when used from top to bottom in attic rooms where the ceiling runs into the wall and there is no natural break.

Veneered panelling is available in many finishes and the price will depend on the type of wood selected. Be sure to buy all the panels from the same batch so that the grain is consistent. A room does not need to be panelled from top to bottom to get the full effect, you could panel beneath the dado rail and paint or wallpaper above it.

PAINTED FINISHES

Paint is quick and versatile and can transform a room instantly, changing its proportions, accentuating its best features and disguising its faults. There are hundreds of different standard colours to choose from. If you can, buy a small trial pot and paint a small section of the wall to make sure that it dries to the colour you think you have chosen from the card.

1

PAINT, FABRIC AND WALLPAPER

1 *Rich coral paintwork is ideal for showing off paintings and antique furniture and makes a good contrast to the panelling below the dado and the woodwork.*

2 *A traditional room, renovated and furnished in period style. On the walls is a red Suedel fabric, which obviously would not have been around in the 18th century, but it shows off the paintings and furniture well and ties in with the existing curtains.*

3 *A ticking stripe fabric has been mounted on these walls. First the walls were battened and interlined, the fabric was then sewn together in measured lengths and stretched onto the battens.*

4 *Another way of putting fabric onto walls is to back it with paper and then stick it to the walls like wallpaper. This is a paper-backed moiré fabric and, like wallpaper, it needs a good smooth surface to adhere to.*
5 *This attic bedroom with an irregular ceiling shape was wallpapered all over,* ceiling as well as walls, in a pretty trellis design. When wallpapering into nooks and crannies it is best to choose a wallpaper with a small all-over pattern like this one, rather than a strong repeat pattern.*

Wonderful effects can be obtained from specialist paint finishes, and you can learn how to apply them yourself with the help of a good book on the subject. But do not get carried away – too much decorative paint-work can be overwhelming. This kind of paintwork is best subtly used to highlight important architectural features such as cornices, panelling and architraves.

WALLPAPER

If you are wondering which to select first – the fabric or the wallpaper – choose the fabric, because generally speaking it is easier to find a wallcovering to match a fabric than vice versa. Most traditional papers are machine printed and come in three main finishes: spongeable, washable and vinyl. Spongeable and washable papers have a coating which allows them to be gently cleaned with mild, soapy water. Vinyl is much tougher and shinier and can be scrubbed and is therefore more suitable for bathroom and kitchens.

Handmade papers are both beautiful and expensive. You will have to order a minimum of about 30 rolls, and be prepared to wait for delivery. There is no point in hanging an expensive paper unless the walls have been well prepared. Ideally, walls should be cross lined (which means the lining paper runs horizontally) and the wallpaper hung professionally, using a paste recommended by the manufacturer.

FABRIC

Fabric looks wonderful on walls. It can disguise any number of blemishes and bumps and will provide insulation against heat loss and noise. Paper-backed fabrics can be stuck directly to smooth walls, as can heavy-weight fabrics that will not stretch.

Alternatively fabric can be stapled onto a framework of battens or stretched over panels of plywood, or shirred onto poles fixed top and bottom. Fabritrack is a useful new system whereby the fabric is tucked into slots and held by an adhesive strip so that it hangs flat.

1

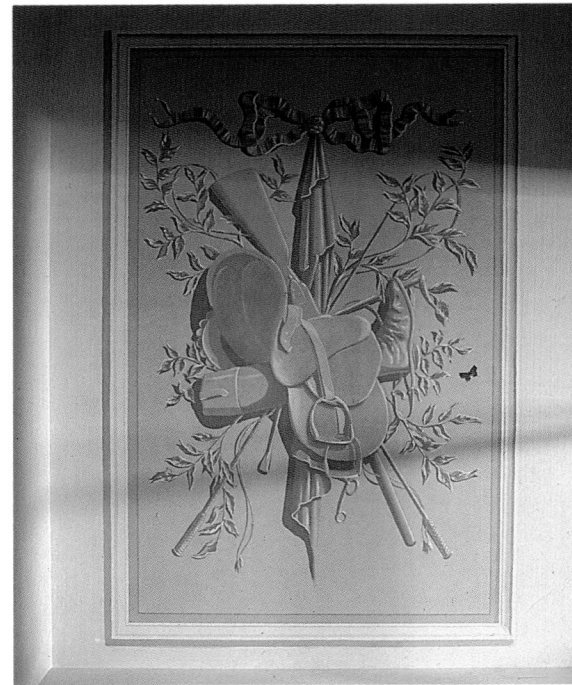

2

MURALS AND PICTURES

1 *A hand-painted Chinese wallpaper, probably about 30 years old, in subtle shades of sepia and grey. A design like this leads the eye into the scene and beyond, giving the room a feeling of depth.*
2 *Trompe l'oeil architectural moulding*

3

5

6

4

on an equine theme painted in a trompe l'oeil panel. The design is picked out in subtle tones of beige and grey and shows how very effective a restrained use of colour can be.

3 A wall of dragged soft beige paintwork is an excellent foil for gilt frames, the rich patina of antique wood

and the toffee-coloured glaze of the Chinese jars.

4 A symmetrical display of smartly-framed architectural prints looks wonderful on this marble-effect chimney breast. Architectural prints can often be picked up for next to nothing in junk shops. Restored and framed they make

a striking wall decoration.

5 & 6 Trompe l'oeil murals painted within an arched framework showing glimpses of outdoor country life. These two murals flank a mirror of similar shape on a wall that has no windows.

FLOORS

Practical considerations come first when choosing a floor-covering, followed by aesthetics and then budget. There is an enormous difference in cost between different grades of carpet and different types of ceramic or wooden floors.

CARPETS AND RUGS

Plain wall-to-wall carpet makes a room feel larger and, if used throughout the house, will provide continuity. Patterned carpets will make a room feel smaller and more intimate – they are a good choice for larger rooms where much of the carpet is exposed to view.

Carpets are expensive, so be sure that you know what you are buying. Cheap synthetic carpet is never a good investment as it stains easily and wears out quickly.

There are basically two main types of carpet pile: cut and looped. Within these divisions there are many variations from velvet cut piles to twisted shag piles. Most woven carpets are produced by Axminster or Wilton, their names deriving from the type of loom on which they are woven. Both produce plain and patterned carpets, the Wilton being the better quality but only able to incorporate a maximum of five colours. An Axminster loom can accommodate up to 35 colours and so Axminsters tend to have more complex and intricate designs.

Berber carpets are made from undyed

1

2

CARPETS AND RUGS

Inset & 1 *Portuguese needlepoint rugs can be specially woven in any colours you desire. These two rugs have been made to the same basic design but in different colours, one complementing the dining room scheme, the other the sitting room.*

3

5

4

6

2 *An old, faded needlepoint rug. These rugs look good on any surface from sisal matting to luxurious carpet.*

3 *A specially commissioned needlepoint rug, made for the dining room at Pusey House, combines strong graphic borders with pretty floral motifs. The hunting horn, which you can see upside down at* the top of the picture, is actually the family crest.

4 *An antique Persian rug with strong colours and a strong graphic design.*

5 *Antique Aubusson rug in wonderful shades of cream, beige and pink. It would look wonderful almost anywhere, but Aubusson rugs look* especially good on gleaming wooden floors.

6 *Rich colours and intricate designs are the hallmark of Persian rugs. They look good with any scheme, classic or modern, pale or dark.*

sheep wool with a thick loop pile. They are practical and good-looking and an ideal base for rugs.

Brussels weave is a tightly looped pile carpet, good for intricate patterns, but it does need to be well laid. Its use on stairs is not recommended, but it does make wonderful dense and colourful rugs.

Matting is a good alternative to carpet and is available in a variety of different finishes. It is durable and looks good in most rooms although it is hard on bare feet in bedrooms. Rugs look particularly good thrown over a base of coir matting.

Basically, a carpet is as good as the fibre it is made from. The best and the most used is 100% wool or a combination of 80% wool and 20% nylon to give added strength. Wool carpets shrug off most stains with remarkable ease and will retain their life and looks for many years if well maintained.

HARD FLOORS

Wooden floors are warm, durable and attractive. Hardwood makes the best flooring but softwood, plywood and chipboard can all be cut and varnished and made to look extremely good.

Stone and tiled floors are generally considered cold and bleak, but used in the right place and laid the right way they can be very effective. Most stone floor finishes are available in slab or tile form. Tiles are generally cheaper although they take more time to lay. Make your choice depending on the size of the room. A large entrance hall, for instance, will look much better with large slabs of stone or slate while a small bathroom would benefit from the smaller scale of the tile.

CORK AND VINYL

Cork tiles and synthetic floor coverings must be correctly laid for the best effect. They are practical, waterproof, durable, warm underfoot and ideal for kitchens, eating areas and bathrooms. A good quality marble or tile design vinyl floor, such as Amtico, looks surprisingly like the real thing, especially when laid with borders.

HARD FLOORS

1 *A herringbone parquet floor, an ideal and practical base for any room, looks particularly good with brightly-coloured rugs.*
2 *Terracotta tiles look warm but they are cold underfoot, so for added warmth put a rug on top. The rug should have*

3

6

4

some sort of backing to stop it slipping dangerously about.

3 *Flagstone floors look wonderful in large, country house hallways. If you are planning to lay a new stone floor, remember the larger the room, the larger the flags should be.*

4 *An old flagstone floor with inset squares of black slate. This floor finish is very common in country houses.*

5 *A checkerboard design of black and red terracotta tiles gives width to a narrow hallway.*

6 *A parquet effect vinyl tiled floor, laid out like a rug with a herringbone central panel and a double border.*

WINDOW DRESSING

1

2

3

On a purely practical level, a window lets in light and air and a curtain or blind provides privacy and doubles as a draught excluder. On an aesthetic level, however, window treatments can make or break a successful room design.

If you have a beautiful window, obviously you have to come up with a treatment that will highlight its best features. A graceful arch, for instance, would be ruined by putting a pole across the top. Equally a really boring window can be made to look perfectly elegant by dressing it up with swagged pelmets or by using a fabric so stunning that the eye is completely deceived.

The choice of window treatment is a major design decision. I have always believed that if you can get the window treatment right, ideas for the rest of the room will fall into place.

GEORGIAN AND PALLADIAN

Georgian windows have the most elegant proportions of all, being tall and fairly narrow. Such windows should not be over-treated or their elegance will be hidden under a welter of pelmets. They look best with full length curtains or with festoon or Roman blinds.

Arched, or Palladian windows – named after the 16th century Italian architect Andrea Palladio – pose a tricky problem. Where possible the arch shape should be

CURTAINS WITH PELMETS
Inset *Tie-back of damask and lace.*
1 *This stiffened pelmet has been taken right up to the ceiling and out to the edge of the bay, its zig-zag edge highlighted with a red edging.*
2 *A stiffened and shaped pelmet that took its cue directly from the pattern.*

3 *This inspired pelmet frames a beautiful view from an upstairs bedroom window. It has been softly gathered and ruched with an edging of stiffened material cut into the shape of leaves echoing the wisteria beyond. The fresh, yellow-green fabric reinforces the feeling of the garden*

coming right into the house.

4 *A grand stiffened and sculpted pelmet with stylish tassels. A sculpted edge is often set off with a contrasting edging.*

5 *These beautiful pinky-red curtains were never designed to be drawn. The pelmet is softly gathered and draped, and behind the pelmet is a peachy-*

cream festoon curtain.

6 *This charming stiffened and shaped lambrequin frames a bathroom window and hides a plain roller blind.*

7 *In the adjoining bedroom, the same fabric is gathered into a softly ruched pelmet, prettily edged in pink and decorated with bows.*

maintained and followed, either by using curtains or a pelmet shaped at the top to follow the arch, or by using a festoon curtain or a shaped shutter.

CASEMENTS, SASHES AND BAYS

Casement windows opening inwards should not be obstructed by curtains. Shutters coupled with dress curtains that do not pull would be one solution, a roller blind attached to the window itself is another.

Sash windows are the easiest to treat as they present no opening restrictions and, if you have sufficient room between the top of the window and the cornice, they can take an interestingly draped pelmet.

Bay windows provide an excellent opportunity for exotic window treatments. They work better if treated as a whole, with the pelmet following the shape of the bay. The main problem with bay windows is in cutting out the light with several sets of curtains that all need somewhere to stack. A solution may be to fix blinds to the individual windows and then dress the frame or wall in front of the bay with curtains.

DORMERS AND SKYLIGHTS

Dormer windows are often best left untreated to let in the maximum amount of light. If curtains are appropriate, they can be fixed on to hinged rods which fold back onto the flanking wall. These are called drapery arms and curtains fitted to them have to be double-sided as the reverse is visible when the rod is folded back against the wall. If privacy is a problem then sheers can be ruched onto poles top and bottom and fixed to the frame.

Skylights are best treated with roller blinds or sheers fixed to the frame. Any small, awkwardly-shaped window is probably best left untreated, but if privacy is a problem obscured glass is probably the best solution.

GARDEN DOORS

French windows opening outwards will not present a problem, but for doors that open

1

2

TIE-BACKS

1 *Plaited tie-back. Three even, hemmed and slightly padded strips of curtain fabric have been plaited, as one would plait one's hair – effective when you want the tie-back to blend in.*

2 *Stiffened tie-back in the same material as the curtain, but trimmed with the*

braid that also decorates its leading edge and finished with a ruffled rosette.

3 Simple tie-backs on a pair of door curtains cleverly placed so that the curtains form a frame for the triangular light above the door and stay well out of the way of the constant opening and shutting.

4 The traditional rope tassel tie-back. In this case the rope and its elegant tassels were specially made to tie in with the braid and the colour of the curtain fabric.

5 Tie-back arms are made from short lengths of pole, covered in fabric with rosettes stuck on the end. These curtains do not draw. By day they are tucked behind the tie-back arms to keep them away from the window and at night the curtains hang straight.

3

4

5

inwards obviously any curtains are going to have to pull back well clear of the window. Curtains should be full length and drawn back onto the side walls to let in the maximum amount of light. If the doors are set back into a deep reveal then it is best to attach curtains to the wall and maybe individual blinds on each window.

Walls that are totally glazed and huge picture windows may be better left untreated. For security, or to shut out the light, a blind or grill could be recessed into the ceiling in a cavity above the window and let down only when necessary.

CURTAINS

The atmosphere and appearance of a room will be changed dramatically by curtaining. It can make a large uninviting room feel cosy or a small room feel claustrophobic. Basically, you have to be prepared to lose a bit of light because no curtain treatment, apart from a drift of transparent muslin on a transparent pole, will increase the feeling of light and space.

Straight curtains are best hung from a pole or curtain track. Poles can be decorative or painted, wooden or brass and either corded or with rings. Tracks, although practical, are unsightly and are often hidden behind a fabric-covered fascia board. Dress curtains are used, as their name suggests, to dress a window. They are not made to draw and they are often embellished with fringes and braids and tassels. They tend to be used in conjunction with other more practical window treatments, such as blinds or shutters, but they can also be used to create a dramatic feature in a room where curtains are not necessary. Dress curtains are generally hung either side of the window opening and held in place with tie-backs.

Another way to dress a window is to swag or drape the fabric over a pole above the window. This was a popular fashion in England in the 17th and 18th centuries.

Cafe curtains hang across the lower part of a sash window, generally fixed to a brass or wooden rod. They give both privacy and

1

2

AWKWARD WINDOWS

1 *A sloping ceiling posed a problem here both for the hanging of pictures and the positioning of the curtain pole. Now they complement each other. At night the curtains, which are on a semi-circular track, are loosened and they fall to cover window and window seat.*

172

5

6

3

4

window so the sill is never obscured.
4 *A window with a bath set right underneath it is an impractical place for curtains. The solution here was a laminated roller blind with a shaped base and a swagged dressing hanging on a pole above.*
5 *A little window with an arched top dressed with a little festoon curtain that follows the arch.*
6 *Festoon curtain on a side window made to match grander curtains on the main window in the same room.*

2 *Curtains on this sloped Velux window are held in at sill level by a fabric covered pole, so they are held firmly against the wall when drawn*

and when pulled back.
3 *A window with a deep recess has dress curtains fixed to the wall and a roller blind in matching material fixed to the*

light at the same time and can look effective in kitchens made up from simple fabrics such as checks or voiles.

On the subject of curtain fabric, I think you get a better effect using more of a cheap fabric than less of an expensive one. It is better to spend money on having the curtains well made. An inexpensive plain cotton beautifully lined and interlined, perhaps with an edging or a trimming and an elegant pelmet looks more effective than an expensive silk, skimpily made.

CURTAIN HEADINGS

A heading is the gathering or pleating at the top of the curtain which determines the way the fabric will fall.

Pinch pleats are rows of hand-sewn pleats grouped generally in threes with a flat area between the groups. They make the curtain fall into rich-looking, natural folds. Goblet headings are made in the same way, but using just one large pleat shaped like a goblet which should be stuffed with interlining to maintain its shape.

Pencil pleats are small continuous pleats created by using a special tape. A pencil pleated curtain will fall into tightly gathered, narrow vertical folds.

Gathered headings are generally used for curtains that will be hidden at the top by a pelmet and they make the fabric fall in a very natural way.

Slot headings are suitable for fixed curtains on a pole. The curtains are ruched onto the pole through a slot sewn into the top.

PELMETS

From simple shapes to exotic swags and tails embellished with fringes and rope, pelmets will enhance any window. Pelmets sit at the top of the window attached to a pelmet board and the track on which the curtains hang is, in turn, attached to the base of the board. The drop of the pelmet will conceal any unsightly curtain tracks as well as the curtain headings.

Pelmets are all about proportion. You can make a window look taller by positioning

1

THE FULL TREATMENT

1 *Beautifully-made curtains in a lovely faded rose patterned chintz hide a simple white roller blind which can be pulled down to protect furnishings and fabrics from the destructive glare of the sun.*

2 *Arched windows, however grand or simple, should have arched pelmets. These ones had existing arched cornices to which the swagged pelmets have been attached. The rope trimmings tie the curtains in with the delicate filigree on the mirrors and the gilded mouldings on walls and ceiling.*

3 *Grand window treatment in which the top of the pelmets have been kept square in keeping with the shape of the windows, but the base of the stiffened pelmets have been shaped to add interest. Again, roller blinds are used to cut out glare.*

4 & 5 *On the bow window, a full blown swag and tail treatment has been carried out in a bold traditional chintz, complete with edging tassels and*

2

4

3

5

rosettes. The room divider curtain is
altogether simpler in design, but it is
made of the same fabric and in much the
same spirit and the two work
beautifully together.

the pelmet board well above the window and you can enhance arched or Gothic windows by following the lines of the window. The proportion of pelmet depth to curtain is very important. I generally allow 2–2$\frac{1}{2}$ inches per foot of curtain drop.

Hard pelmets can be made of wood that has been shaped and then painted, or of stiffened fabric such as buckram which is then covered with fabric. Soft pelmets or valances are made of lined and interlined fabric, shaping the base line or adding a frill or contrast edge to give definition.

Lambrequins are stiff, fabric-covered wooden pelmets with long sides which form a casing to a window. They look good with blinds behind them rather than curtains and are good for deep set windows or windows with little space on either side.

The most elaborate pelmet of all is the swags and tails which of course does not suit every style of window. It works best on tall windows with full length curtains. To work well, swags and tails must look full and rich, and the width of the window will govern how many swags to use.

BLINDS

An excellent alternative to curtains, blinds are extremely practical. They can be used with curtains or on their own, they require a great deal less fabric but can be equally decorative.

Roller blinds can be made up from virtually any fabric that has been stiffened or laminated. They are ideal in areas where curtains would get in the way.

Roman blinds are formed by a simple cording system. When down they appear flat like roller blinds, and when up they fall into a series of horizontal folds.

Austrian blinds hang straight when let down but when pulled up on their vertical cords they balloon into soft folds. Festoon blinds are fuller and fussier than Austrian blinds, when let down they remain ballooned. They are often frilled and edged and bound on all sides and are best used on their own, rather than with curtains.

1

2

1 *Stiffened, shaped pelmets, elegantly trimmed with rope and fringing. The wooden shutters are closed at night so that the window seats and alcoves, formed by the window recesses, can still be used.*

3

4

5

2 *Simple and elegant. The plain silk curtains run on a track and the pelmet effect is achieved by draping a length of fringed fabric on a pole to simulate swags and tails.*

3 *Large bay window dressed with three*

pairs of cream silk curtains that draw individually, on each part of the bay. The swags and tails pelmet is made as one and fitted onto a pole shaped to follow the line of the bay.

4 & 5 *Full length curtains on recessed*

sash windows. One has plain dress curtains and a stiffened pelmet fitted on the outside edge of the reveal and patterned curtains close to the window, the other has gathered curtains on the wall and shutters to close at night.

Upholstered Seating

There are endless styles of sofas, armchairs, wing chairs, side chairs and ottomans available, antique and new. The ideal treatment varies according to the piece, its use and location, but prime factors in selecting both the seat and its cover should be comfort and practicality.

THE UPHOLSTERY

Many people tend to ignore the construction of a chair or sofa and concentrate on the top cover. However it is the upholstery attached to the frame that gives the basic shape.

Antique chairs that have, over the years, been re-upholstered to keep up with current trends or to make them more comfortable have probably altered out of all recognition. A good upholsterer will be able to match chairs or alter their shapes providing the frame is in good condition.

Well-upholstered seating is worth paying for. Earlier this century the introduction of foam padding meant that traditional upholstery skills were no longer essential for modern products and the role of the old-fashioned upholsterer was limited to restoring antique pieces. Recently, however, strict new fire regulations have meant that more and more upholsterers and manufacturing companies are being forced to revert to traditional methods of upholstery. Although this does mean an increase in costs, it also means a better quality product which will be

CUSHIONS

Inset *Daffodil yellow cushion on a mustard yellow chair – the colours are taken from the wallpaper.*
1 *Selection of cushions made from antique fabrics. The old pieces of fabric need not necessarily be cushion-sized – the cushion in the foreground has a new*

damask cover and a band of antique embroidery edged in braid.

2 Needlepoint cushion with added embroidery picks up and enhances the colour of the sofa.

3 Cushions in the same fabric as the upholstery look effective when interspersed with others.

4 A little work of art, hand-embroidered with silk on a plain cotton background.

5 A rich red sofa enlivened with richly-decorated cushions. These are fringed damask cushions with bands of patterned damask.

6 A stencilled cushion and two chintz ones in complementary colours.

more comfortable and last a lot longer.

There are many manufacturers producing a whole range of modern and traditional designs upholstered in a variety of ways. Do not choose seating from a catalogue without sitting on it before you part with your money, as looks can be deceptive.

Do check the dimensions. One three-seater sofa can be a foot smaller or larger than another and often the so-called matching armchairs will appear hugely out of proportion so it may be necessary to order smaller ones. Also take into account the delivery, especially in town, as many staircases and doorways are just too small to allow passage of a large sofa.

Most sofas have seat cushions, but not all of them have back cushions. A fixed padded back without cushions will give you a more formal, tailored look, while back cushions look more casual and comfortable.

THE COVERS

Virtually any fabric can be used for upholstery, but obviously some are more suitable and will last longer than others. The one essential is that all upholstery fabrics should pass the cigarette and match test. Your supplier will advise you on this point.

Your choice is between loose covers and fixed. If a chair or sofa has an interesting shape, then a tight cover should be used, as a loose cover will hide the detail. Fabrics can always be Scotchguarded or Fibre Sealed to help prevent the penetration of dust and grime, and where heavy use is anticipated, arm caps and head caps can provide extra protection. Cushion covers should always be zipped so they can be removed for cleaning.

Loose covers are more suitable for simple forms of armchairs and sofas. They are practical but not so elegant as they will eventually lose their shape. If you require a loose cover, then the sofa or armchair will be covered firstly in calico and the cover will be cut and fitted on top. If you can't make a decision on the fabric, you can always live with the calico for a while, and drape fabric over it until inspiration strikes.

SOFAS AND CHAIRS

1 *A traditional armchair with a tight chintz cover, contrast piped to highlight the shape of the chair. The silk-screen printed cushion has a fan edge in pink and white to match the chintz.*
2 *Sofa with back and seat cushions upholstered in a striped cotton velvet*

5

6

3

4

and piped in the same fabric. The
feet are hidden with a thick, cream
bullion fringe.

3 A wonderful deep-buttoned chaise
longue upholstered in chintz and velvet
and eccentrically trimmed with ornate
tassels.

4 Modern sofas with interestingly-
shaped backs – an important
consideration if the sofas are to be
freestanding in the room.

5 An old church pew made more
comfortable for dining with a cushion
and a box-pleated skirt.

6 An interesting little ottoman with
bolsters at each end, tightly upholstered
and edged with rope. To emphasize the
shape of the bolsters, a contrast circle of
plain red has been inset.

SIDE CHAIRS

1 *Walnut and mahogany side chair from Blenheim Palace. It is upholstered with antique needlework and finished with* brass studs.

2 *Antique upholstered settee with turned legs and stretchers in mahogany. The beautiful antique tapestry is* finished with old braid.

3 *Pretty painted armchair with upholstered, partly padded arms for added comfort.*

5

7

6

8

4 Oval-backed, painted and gilded armchair with a buttoned back. The fabric has been finished in braid.

5 Painted and gilded armchair upholstered with a hand-embroidered shell design fabric and finished with brass studs.

6 Gilt armchair with a padded back and loose seat cushion, finished with braid rather than studs.

7 Painted and gilded armchair with seat and back upholstered in hand-embroidered tapestry. The upholstery panels are inset into the chair and so require neither braid nor studs.

8 French reproduction fauteuil in pickled pine smartly upholstered in a green and red fabric, in keeping with the overall colour scheme and the polished wooden floor.

COFFEE TABLES AND FOOTSTOOLS

A period coffee table is impossible to find. They are a very recent requirement and so called 'reproductions' look painfully out of place in the classic interior, while modern designs are not always suitable. A good solution is to use an old panel or tray of antique lacquer or *papier mâché* and have a base constructed for it, perhaps of wood made to simulate bamboo and painted in a colour to match the tray.

Lacquered pieces can, in fact, make very attractive coffee tables. An old Chinese chest or a simple table painted in an antique lacquered finish would be perfectly in keeping, and there are quite a few companies who specialize in this treatment.

Glass-topped coffee tables are often used when a feeling of space is required. Choose these with care. A lot of them are made with chromium-plated or brass fittings and have a very clinical air about them and sharp edges which are not a good idea if there are young children about.

A popular alternative to the coffee table is the upholstered stool covered in an antique rug to provide a hard-wearing, attractive finish. These work well as they provide comfortable extra seating as well as a firm base for a tray of drinks.

Footstools are an attractive accessory. Long narrow ones placed in front of a fireplace double as a fender, and small round ones often come in handy as doorstops.

1

2

Inset *An old footrest with mahogany bun feet covered in a hand-embroidered tapestry in lovely autumn hues.*
1 *A beautiful antique footstool with petit point needlework in many subtle colours. It is a fine piece of work that goes very well with the antique tapestry rug on which it sits.*

3

5

4

6

2 *This firmly upholstered footstool-cum-coffee table is a modern piece covered in a tapestry-type fabric and edged with studs.*

3 *A stunning fringe hides the sides of this beautifully upholstered stool, giving it a more formal air.*

4 *A conventional, oriental-style*

wooden coffee table that has been painted in a distressed finish in two tones of pink with gilt borders. The glass top is there to protect the paintwork.

5 *A modern stool with turned mahogany legs has been upholstered in a kelim. Its firm surface makes it*

perfectly suitable for use as a coffee table.

6 *Turkish fabric has been used to cover this attractively-shaped antique stool that is large enough to double as a table and hold a tray of drinks.*

FIREPLACES

The introduction of central heating has seen the demise of many a beautiful fireplace. Fortunately 'the trend is now towards reinstating the fireplace as an architectural feature – to act as a focal point as well as to provide welcome back-up heat.

When opening up an old fireplace, the flue must be carefully checked to make sure that it is in working order. Some flues may require a special liner if a stove or gas fire is to be used. All fires require a stone, marble or brick hearth and they should be installed by specialists or by builders who understand the complexities of fire and smoke.

The choice of surround will depend on the style and period of the house. It is important that the surround is in proportion to the room and the chimney breast on which it will be located. Surrounds are generally made from wood, marble or stone. Wooden ones are generally neat and flat and can be polished or painted in any way to suit any colour scheme. Marble surrounds range from the simple to the ornate. Old marble is expensive and should always be professionally installed. Stone fireplaces tend to be simple yet massive and are best suited to large fireplaces in country houses.

There is nothing less inviting than an empty fireplace. If no fire is burning in the grate, fill the space with plants or dried flowers or put an attractive firescreen in front to hide the black hole.

1

Inset *Conventional symmetry – a fabulous timepiece flanked by dogs.*
1 A magnificent marble fireplace commands attention. Here the soft beige of the walls and the lovely faded pinks and blues of the carpet set it off to perfection.
2 A wooden fire surround, simply

2

4

6

3

5

painted in white, has marble hearth and slips and a useful club fender to provide additional occasional seating.

3 Not as medieval as it seems, this carved stone fireplace is about 80 years old. The oversized fireirons are perfectly in keeping.

4 A wooden reproduction fireplace is given a grander feeling with a strong symmetrical arrangement of figurines that emphasize the outer edges rather than the centre.

5 An elegantly simple white marble fireplace set into a flat wall. The mirror above it is framed with period mouldings and painted in a marble effect finish to match the fireplace, thus giving the effect of a chimney breast.

6 Grey marble surrounds an open fire and is beautifully set off by the soft scumbled paint on the walls.

COLLECTIONS

A collection should reflect your own interests. It doesn't have to be a clutch of priceless Fabergé eggs, just a group of related objects that will give you lasting pleasure. Good-looking displays can emerge from collections of objects as mundane as old tins or as esoteric as cow-shaped cream jugs.

It is the way in which you display your collection that will give it impact. There are a few basic ground rules to bear in mind. Keep the collection well focused and do not try and cram too many different kinds of objects together, or it will cease to be a collection and become a mess of bits and pieces without impact.

Beware of collecting objects that are too easy to find because, unless you have iron self-control, you will find yourself swamped with stuff. Light the collection well, especially if you are displaying pictures, and every time you add to your collection, check to see if something needs taking out.

The most obvious display area for objects is shelving. Check at what height your collection is best appreciated, as some objects look best side on, and some have to be seen from above. Some things look better on glass shelves and others on a pine dresser. Small precious items might be better off in a well-lit glass case, protected from children and animals. Experiment until you find the ideal home and setting for your particular brand of treasures.

BIRD'S EYE VIEW
Inset *A restrained collection of silver boxes given a focal point by a Japanese figurine.*
1 *An antique lace cloth, protected by glass, shows off a varied collection of porcelain doves.*
2 *A precise arrangement of old and new*

188

3

6

4

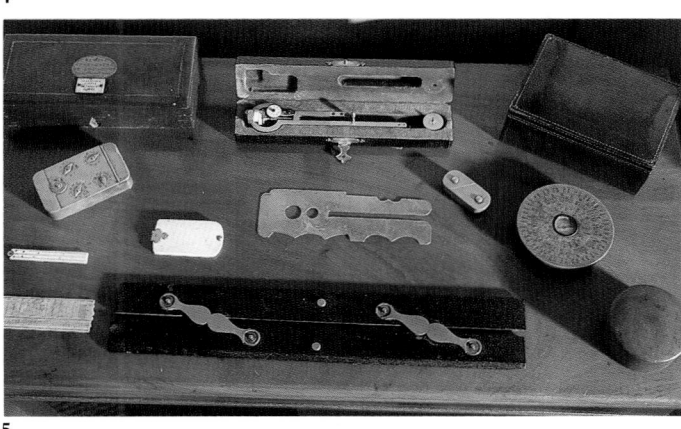

5

enamel boxes and marble eggs.

3 *A wonderful collection of old ivory objets d'art beautifully displayed on a restrained background of donkey brown velour.*

4 *Painted antique snuff boxes with a rich golden patina which is echoed in the wooden surround of the antique leather-topped table.*

5 *Antique navigational equipment laid out shipshape fashion on an old mahogany side table.*

6 *A display of beautifully polished silver boxes on a beautifully polished table. Collections such as these do need a lot of maintenance to look their best.*

SHELVES AND TABLETOPS

1 *In a room of almost unbelievable blues, blue painted shelves hold a collection of blue and white antique Chinese porcelain.*

2 *An antique console table is home to a display of thick Biot glass and a pair of porcelain figures.*

3 *A priceless collection of antique French vases interspersed with tiny dried flower trees enhance the wonderful golden tones of an Impressionist painting.*

4 *A very 18th century mode of display – tiny purpose-built shelves hold single Chinese porcelain bowls.*

5 *Blue and white English willow pattern china given a touch of humour with the introduction of a suitably patterned cow.*

6 *An eclectic mix of leather-bound books, decanters, antique telescopes and butterflies show how effective such a diverse collection can be.*

4

5

6

STORAGE

For most of us, storage space is something we always need more of. This applies particularly to town houses or flats where space is limited. You can make the most of what storage you have by customizing the interiors of all your cupboards from wardrobes to workboxes. Plan logically, storing items as near as possible to where they will be used and allow easy access. It is all very well having a huge attic or cellar but they are not places you can store items you will need frequently.

Everyone needs clothes storage consisting of hanging space, shelves or drawers. Work out the proportion of hanging space requirements to shelving, and then decide how much short length hanging space you need as you can double up and save space.

In the kitchen, try and plan the storage in separate areas. Keep food, pots and pans, glasses and crockery next to the area where they will be first used.

Coats and boots and prams are difficult to store in a small house or flat. If you can't find room for a separate cupboard then a row of hooks will have to suffice.

When building in cupboards, do make sure that they are well lit, well ventilated and most important of all, deep enough. Check the measurements of a jacket on a hanger before you do anything, and always build cupboards up to the ceiling, as the top can be used for seasonal items or suitcases.

1

2

Inset *A bedroom cupboard heavily disguised with wallpaper and a pair of floral prints.*
1 *An effective way to make a large expanse of cupboard doors look interesting. Prints have been inset into the panels of these brightly painted doors, mounted on squares of*

3

5

6

4

practically disappears into the wall
thanks to a coat of paint and a piece of
matching skirting board.
4 Wonderful example of how to use that
lost space over the door – here it has
been incorporated into a wall of books.
5 A good example of shelving of
different depths that has been built into
an awkward corner making the best use
of limited space.
6 A painted and stencilled dresser where
the requirement for storage space meets
the requirement for display space to
great effect.

marbled wallpaper.
2 An antique free-standing wardrobe of
generous proportions decorated with a

distressed paint finish and hand-painted
motifs in every panel.
3 Simple wooden shelving that

CAMOUFLAGE

Many items essential to modern life do not fit well into classic decorating schemes, and this is where a bit of disguise and deception come in. The most obvious eyesore is the radiator. These can be boxed in with a wooden frame and a grille without losing heat. In a hall or narrow passageway, the casing itself can become quite an attractive feature, as well as providing a useful shelf. Under a window the casing can become part of a window seat and, if the radiator is set into an alcove, the casing can form part of a bookcase.

Where boxing-in would be impractical, paint the radiators in the same finish as the wall and you probably won't notice them at all, apart from the fact that they protrude from the wall. With advance planning radiators can disappear into recesses in the wall.

The television set is another common eyesore. One solution is to hide it under a skirted table which has curtains that draw back easily on tracks or swing out of the way on hinged arms. It could be sunk into a wall at eye level or into a disused chimney breast and hidden behind a picture, or kept inside a cupboard on a special pivoting bracket so it can be tilted into a good viewing position.

Modern stereo equipment is, in general, smart and good looking enough to stack into a bookcase, and speakers are now so narrow that it is possible to conceal them in walls, ceiling cavities or radiator casings.

1

2

3

4

Inset *A ceiling-hung curtain over a doorway hides the fuse box. The high tie-back ensures the curtain doesn't get in the way.*

1 *An antique painted screen in a bedroom is useful for hiding all sorts of clutter that is waiting to find its way back to the wardrobe.*

2 *Underneath the round table is a TV set and a video. The red velvet cloth is in fact a pair of curtains that draw back easily on a track.*

3 *A typical radiator casing with cane grilles that has been incorporated in a window seat. There is a narrow grille at the back of the seat cushion to allow for airflow.*

4 *A solid and beautifully crafted old French armoire transformed by the decorative paint expert, Laurience Rogier. The trompe l'oeil books are covered with real chicken wire to give an even more disturbingly realistic effect to the piece.*

HALLS AND STAIRS

The hall gives the first impression of a home and it is important that it exudes a warm, welcoming atmosphere. In town houses or flats a hall is generally no more than a narrow passage leading to a flight of stairs. If ceilings are high and there is a lack of natural light, the effect can be tunnel-like. One simple solution is to open up the room adjacent to the entrance by installing double doors or an archway. Not only will this increase the feeling of space, it will also let in the light. If removing walls is out of the question, then mirrors, good lighting and a few decorative tricks can help make narrow halls feel wider and lighter.

Generally speaking, the hall of a country house is probably large enough to be treated as a room, but a room with specific functions. It is there to protect the rest of the house from outside elements such as draughts and muddy footprints and must also house coats and boots and umbrellas. The floor surface should be durable and easy to clean. Stone flags are ideal, but any hard floor finish will suffice.

Whatever the decorative theme of the hall it should, generally speaking, flow on up the stairs. Staircases take a lot of wear and tear and require a good quality carpet and a sensible finish on the walls. Finally, plan the lighting well. Lights should be positioned so they shine onto the stair treads. A two-way switch system is a must.

Inset *A striking mural draws the eye up the stairs.*
1 *A town house hallway painted a warm and welcoming yellow with a huge mirror to reflect the light.*
2 *A tiny hall in a country cottage given a suitably rustic air with stone flags, a simple umbrella stand and a wicker*

3

5

4

basket full of kindling.

3 A stone-flagged entrance hall, painted white to reflect as much light as possible, gets its imposing feeling from statues in niches and huge Chinese ginger jars.

4 A country house hall that is big enough to be treated as a room. The vivid yellow gives the room instant appeal. The unusual stair rail transforms the staircase, taking away all its bulk and heaviness, giving a feeling of airy lightness to the whole house.

5 In a narrow town house hall the floor tiles are echoed in the carpet design, giving coherence and style to a confined space.

KITCHENS

The priority here is a room that is functional, serviceable and pleasant to be in. Its layout will depend on its size and role. A small room obviously has to be planned as a working kitchen with no eating area. A large one can be treated as a family room serving many needs, although there is one function I think the kitchen can do without if possible, and that is washing and ironing clothes. A separate utility room for washing machines, coats and boots is more practical.

Ideally the kitchen should be divided into separate but linked areas for cooking, washing up, food storage and storage of cooking and eating utensils. Kitchen layout is basically logic and need not require the skills of a specialist kitchen designer. Whoever designs your kitchen, what you will need is work space and plenty of it. Additional work space can be gained by having a table in the centre of the room or pull-out surfaces set under the work top. Food storage, cooker and sink should be within easy reach of one another as these three work stations form the 'work triangle' around which most kitchen layouts are based.

There are endless styles and finishes of kitchen units available as well as custom-built ones and your choice will depend on the look you are trying to create. Obviously wood will give a more traditional country look while shiny melamine and stainless steel will evoke a modern high tech style.

1

2

198

3

4

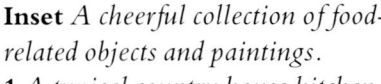

5

6

7

Inset *A cheerful collection of food-related objects and paintings.*
1 *A typical country house kitchen – distinctly unfitted.*
2 *Dresser shelves, attractively crammed*

with assorted china.
3&4 *Examples of custom-built wooden kitchens that look as if they had been put together from a matching collection of free-standing pieces. Such kitchens are expensive but what you get for your money is an unfitted look with all the convenience of modern kitchen design.*

5 *Efficient, tiny and cheerful.*
6 *The farmhouse feeling is reinforced by the soft creams and greens and the apparent lack of modern gadgetry.*
7 *A kitchen with character. The circle motif on the handpainted tiles is repeated by the hanging pans and pot lids and the display of plates.*

DINING AREAS

Bearing in mind the hectic pace of life today, and the fact that many women are choosing to follow a career as well having a family, the trend in the home is towards functional simplicity. In consequence the separate dining room – a room more often than not wasted except for family parties and formal occasions – is now rather over-shadowed by the eat-in kitchen.

A large open plan area which serves the purpose of kitchen, television room, play-room and dining room means that the family will see more of one another. If the kitchen is simply too small to accommodate anything bigger than a breakfast bar, you could consider gaining extra space by adding a conservatory or garden room. Obtaining planning permission for a conservatory is usually a simple procedure, as glass build-ings are not considered to be 'habitable' rooms which frees them from a lot of red tape and building regulations. This does not mean to say that any old lean-to will do. Cutting corners on quality will result in a massive heat loss.

If there is nowhere to dine other than part of the living room, you could make the table double as a work area or invest in a drop leaf table positioned against a wall to save space, and a simple folding screen. On formal oc-casions, a crisp white damask tablecloth, candles, flowers and the sparkle of quality cutlery will focus all attention on the table.

1

2

Inset *A ceramic table centrepiece of undoubted appeal.*
1 *Just in case – this elegantly attired table is suitable for intimate dinners when the dining room seems too large and the kitchen too homely.*
2 *In the corner of a stone-flagged hall a dining table is set up to take advantage of spectacular views and proximity to the kitchen. The table expands to accommodate larger numbers.*
3 *In the hallway of a tiny flat, a swivel top table folds flat against the wall when not in use. The mirrored corner cupboard helps to reflect light into the room and make it seem larger than it is.*

3

5

4

6

4 *Another hallway setting made welcoming with silver and antique lace. During the day the painted wooden table lives in the tiny kitchen and the attractive painted chairs are distributed*

around the house.

5 *Overlooking the garden, this room doubles as dining room and study. When the guests have gone, the table becomes a work area.*

6 *A table set for dinner at one end of a large living room. With the table beautifully laid and the lighting dimmed the rest of the room just melts into the shadows.*

BEDROOMS

The most important criterion for a bedroom is that it should be relaxing and comfortable. It is a room to escape to and forget about the outside world and therefore its atmosphere should reflect such a mood. On the practical side it may well have to double up with some other function, such as a work room and more often than not as a dressing room, so bear this in mind when planning the space.

The first thing you have to do is decide where to put the bed and then plan the rest of the room around it. In a small room you may not have much choice, but if you do have space to play with, think of the view you will get when lying in bed and allow plenty of room for bedside tables.

HEADBOARDS

For comfort, choose a fabric-covered padded headboard – these can be plainly upholstered or bordered with contrast piping and they come in many different shapes. Wooden-framed headboards can have a padded centre for comfort or an inset piece of cane work which can be painted or stained. Brass bedheads are decorative, but be sure to have plenty of comfortable cushions.

VALANCES AND BEDSPREADS

The purpose of a bed valance is to hide the base of the bed. Like pelmets they can be as fancy or as plain as you like. They can be

BEDS WITH DRAPES

Inset *A rosette of stiffened fabric holds back a voile bed curtain.*
1 *A theatrical corona supporting heavy silk curtains lined with printed cotton transforms an ordinary divan bed.*
2 *Plain bed curtains smartened up with a border of chintz.*

3

5

4

3 *This beautiful antique mahogany four-poster has been curtained in a Colefax and Fowler chintz and lined with Fancy Lining. All the curtains have a fan edge in two tones of pink and cream. The ceiling of the bed has been tented with a rosette in the middle, the pleats fanning out to the edges.*

4 *A simple corona for a single bed consisting of a length of chintz that has been carefully lined and pinned into place with three fabric rosettes.*

5 *This delicately shaped antique four-poster has been upholstered in a Spencer-Churchill Designs fabric* Henrietta, *and edged in a plain green chintz. The lining fabric from Charles Hammond is called* Glenalmond *and the ceiling of the bed is a starburst of pleats. The pelmet has been made to follow the curved line of the top to emphasize its elegant curves.*

straight and smart with kick pleats at the corners, or box pleated or gathered and edged and piped and frilled.

Bedspreads can be of the plain throwover variety or tailored to fit. A quilted bedspread not only looks rich and comfortable, it will provide additional warmth and can be made up in any fabric. Cotton throwover bedspreads are practical as they can easily be washed and put back. Antique lace bedspreads give a fresh, clean look and they can always be backed with a coloured lining to make them less fragile.

CORONAS AND HALF-TESTERS

A corona is a circular or semi-circular frame fixed to the ceiling over the bed from which curtains hang around the head of the bed and to the sides, tied back with arms or tie-backs. A half-tester is the same thing, except the frame is rectangular or square. Bed curtains look good made up in the same fabric as the window curtains lined with plain fabric, or a smaller co-ordinating design.

FOUR POSTERS

The most elegant and flamboyant bed of all is the four-poster. They do not have to be museum pieces hung with dusty tapestries. There are many modern four-posters with delicate metal frames or simple wooden ones that look good with all kinds of fabric treatments, from the dark, cosy and womb-like to the simple and fresh sprigged cotton. Unfortunately, most town houses do not have rooms large enough for double four-posters and they are generally more suited to country houses where the proportions are more appropriate.

DAY-BEDS

For rooms that are not specifically bedrooms, but rather rooms with occasional beds in them, the day-bed is a good solution. The bed can be placed against the wall and treated as a sofa with bolsters and cushions. Alternatively a padded headboard and footboard of the same height will give the impression of soft arms.

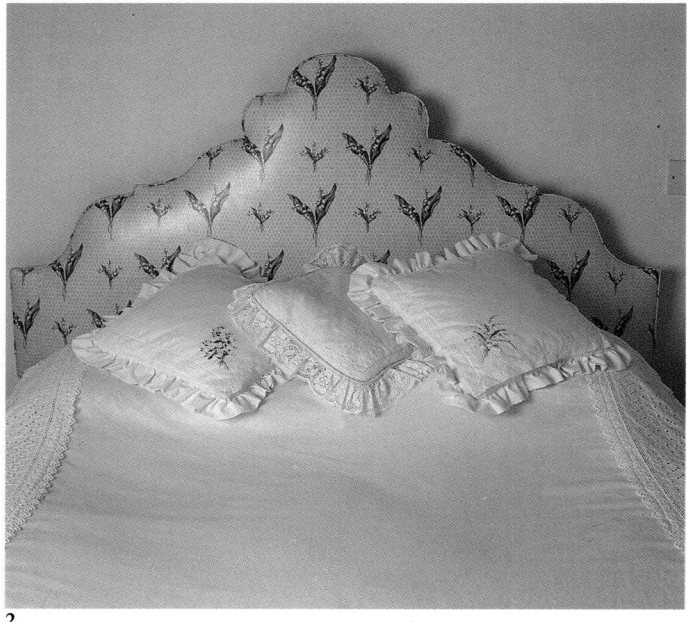

HEADBOARDS AND BEDSPREADS

1 *This smartly upholstered headboard has been teamed with white lace and embroidery.*
2 *The curvaceous headboard has been upholstered in Spencer-Churchill Designs fabric, Consuelo.*

3

3 *An heirloom of a bedspread in subtle, muted colours. Each motif has been cut out and hand-stitched on to a cream silk panel which, in turn, has been stitched to blue silk backing.*

1

2

3

4

SINGLE BEDS AND DAY-BEDS

1 *A tailored chintz loose cover and three smartly upholstered back cushions turn this spare guest bed into a comfortable and useful sofa.*

2 *One way to lighten and soften the effect of heavy-looking wooden head and footboards is to upholster them. This bed has been completely upholstered in chintz and the lovely curvaceous lines have been emphasized with pink piping.*

3 *An antique painted child's bed is well complemented with an old throwover patchwork cover in faded, muted colours.*

4 *A built-in space-saving solution in a tiny guest bedroom that allows the rest of the room to be kept free of bulky wardrobes and chests of drawers.*

5 *This antique day-bed with its graciously curved cane ends is*

beautifully upholstered and comfortably cushioned. The fan-edged mattress cover stops short of covering the carved sides and legs so that the elegant frame can be fully appreciated.

6 The cue for the treatment of this bed has been taken from the smartly striped fabric on the walls. The cane headboard has been painted in a complementary way using colours that exactly match the fabric and the stripe motif has been reprised, but to a different scale, in one of the cushions.

7 This smart guest bedroom-cum-reading corner is in a small mezzanine room off the stairway of a London terraced house. The smart stripes have been used on wall, window and bed in order to turn the sleeping platform area into a cohesive alcove.

5

6

7

BATHROOMS

Unless you are very lucky, your bathroom is probably the smallest room in the house and as such it requires very careful planning. If you are starting from scratch you should first make a list of all your requirements. Do you, for instance, want a bath and a separate shower? Does the WC need to be in the bathroom, or can it be separate? Do you require a bidet? Do you want a pedestal basin or a built-in vanitory unit? Where will you keep towels, shampoos and shaving gear?

BASIC PLANNING

Having established your requirements, you then have to decide where to put everything in order to allow as much space as possible to move around. There are a few basic guidelines that may help you. Locating the WC is the first problem. Because of the complex plumbing involved, you may have very little choice in the matter of its position, but there are quite a few different sizes of WC available, from modern low-level types with slim-line cisterns or flush tanks that can be built into a false wall to full-blown Victorian reproductions with high-level cisterns, and porcelain handles.

Where possible, basins should not be positioned under windows where there is no wall space for a mirror. If, however, that is the only location available, then you could replace a section of the window glass with

Inset *Mirror on mirror: a wall-mounted chrome shaving mirror for those vital close-ups.*
1 *A peach-coloured bathroom sheds a flattering glow on skin tones and the mirrored wall doubles the size of the room and reflects light.*
2 *In this tiny bathroom, mirror glass*

3

5

4

6

has been used in the corner above the vanitory unit. The lights above the mirror create perfect conditions for shaving and making up.

3 This bathroom is in an awkwardly-shaped loft with a domed circular skylight. From the bath one can enjoy spectacular views of the sky.

4 Cream and green give this lovely bathroom an air of the 1930s. Its charm extends to the WC, which has been fitted under the wooden armchair to the left of the basin.

5 This is a bathroom-cum-dressing room in a country house where space is not a problem. The warm yellow walls

and the soft beige carpet make it a warm and inviting environment.

6 Flattering pink walls and a practical marble-effect Corian bathroom suite are given a sense of dignity by the mirrored arches which are framed with wooden architraves artfully painted to resemble pink-veined marble.

mirror or position an anglepoise shaving mirror on a nearby wall.

Whatever style of bath, shower and basin you choose, they should be well sealed and it is always wise to have a course of tiles or marble to protect the walls.

PRACTICAL CONSIDERATIONS

Lighting and heating should be safe and functional. You should use only recommended appliances and have them professionally installed. A heated towel rail is essential and it can either be plumbed into the hot water system providing heat all year round, or switched separately. Make sure it is located within easy reach of the bath or shower. Ventilation is important and, if the bathroom has no window, mechanical ventilation on a time switch should be provided.

The choice of fittings is large, but personally I think if you stick to white you cannot go wrong. Avoid acrylic plastic baths as they will scratch and mark and will not last as long as cast iron. Taps and shower fittings are available in a variety of finishes, chrome and brass being the most popular. If you choose brass, then get them treated with a non-tarnish finish or you will spend a lot of time with a polishing cloth.

The choice of flooring will very much depend on the size and use of the bathroom. Carpet will give warmth to a bathroom but it is not practical if it is to be subjected to constant soaking by children or a shower. Ceramic or marble tiles look good but they are cold underfoot and if laid on a wooden floor they may move and crack. A good alternative is linoleum or Amtico flooring which is good-looking, practical and pleasant to walk on.

If you are fortunate enough to have a large bathroom then it can double up as a dressing room with cupboard storage for clothes, a comfortable armchair and maybe a dressing table for make-up.

Every bathroom should have at least one wall of mirror, essential for reflecting the light and for making what is normally a cramped room feel larger and airier.

1

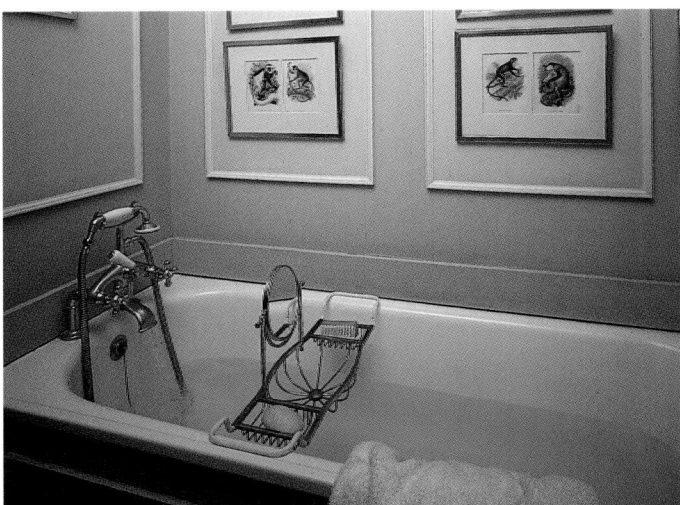

2

3

THE DETAILS

1 *A wonderful view is guaranteed from this bath which faces the window and has been built in with a usefully wide surround which in turn forms the vanitory unit. The focal point in this bathroom is the window. It has a fabric-covered lambrequin edged with a double frill which hides the fixings of a suitably floral roller blind.*

2 *For shaving in the bath, an old fashioned brass bath shelf which matches the solid reproduction brass and porcelain mixer tap.*

3 *Wide tiled shelves beside the bath are a luxury from both a decorative and a practical point of view.*

4 *A bathroom on a rosy theme in which the starkness of the mirrored wall has been given light relief with the addition of an ornate glass and gilt frame fixed to the mirror.*

5 *The bathroom as a picture gallery. The architectural prints have been suitably mounted on blue to match the tiles and well sealed at the back to prevent moisture creeping in. Note the position of the heated rail which keeps towels within easy reach – no need to drip across this bathroom to search for a towel.*

LIGHTING

Most people think of lighting in terms of artificial light, forgetting that natural light should also figure in the lighting plan. If lack of light is a problem or enlarging your existing windows or knocking through some new ones is a problem, then be sure not to drown out the light you have got with pelmets that cover half the window or elaborate curtain treatments that encroach on the glazing area. Most useful light comes in the top half of the window.

Sunlight can be a problem if you have too much of it. It is destructive to furniture, fabrics and carpets. Translucent roller blinds are the best solution. They are neat and unobtrutive when rolled up, and they let a soft, diffused and harmless light through when pulled down.

PLANNING

When planning rewiring from scratch you should consider the function of the room, the position of furniture and architectural features and the overall ambience that you wish to create.

Lighting should be kept as flexible as possible. Any extra sockets, pendant or wall light positions that you wire in at this stage will save later additions which would undoubtedly involve costly decorative work.

To achieve the greatest amount of flexibility within one room, run different types of lighting from separate circuits. This will

1

2

TABLE LAMPS

Inset *Antique Chinese porcelain vase base with a silken shade.*
1 *Terracotta urn-shaped lamp on a base of wood and gilt with a knife-pleated silk shade.*
2 *Italian copy of a tôle candelabra used here with candles. Tôle is a type of*

5

6

3

4

painted ironware.

3 *This magnificent marble table lamp has been raised to floor lamp status thanks to a matching pair of old leather-bound books.*

4 *An ornately carved antique marble urn has been converted into a table lamp with a green lacquered shade. The shade has been painted gold inside to throw a warm light onto the creamy marble.*

5 & 6 *When choosing shades for table lamps, the important consideration is proportion. If the lamp is to be made from a beautiful vase or urn, the bottom of the shade should stop just above the top of the vase so that its shape can be appreciated. These box-pleated silk lampshades top a tôleware urn and a hand-painted porcelain vase.*

enable you to alter the atmosphere in the room quite dramatically. For example, downlighters in the ceiling may be operated from one or two circuits or even more, lamps from another and wall lights from yet another. If they are all on dimmers you will have even more versatility.

GENERAL LIGHTING

There are basically three main kinds of lighting. General lighting is the provision of overall light to a room. In most cases this means a single pendant light hanging from the centre of a room, which does not deliver much in terms of atmosphere. Recessed downlighters or tracks and spots used with dimmers create a softer and much more agreeable effect.

TASK LIGHTING

As its name suggests, task lighting is used to highlight specific areas used for specific tasks, such as reading, working or cooking. It is also used to highlight bookshelves, pictures or collections. It should be precise and reflect true colours and not cause glare or reflection.

Offices, desks or reading areas need good general light, highlighted with desk lamps, or standard lamps that can be angled to suit. Architectural features or pictures can either be individually highlighted with picture lights or by angled spotlights. Fluorescent lamps are a good way to highlight kitchen work surfaces or the inside of cupboards, but the fittings themselves are ugly and should be hidden behind a baffle.

DECORATIVE LIGHTING

Having illuminated the room and provided highlights where needed, you then have the luxury of lighting purely for effect. You can choose from chandeliers, wall lights, uplighters or even a cluster of candles. You can even buy an illuminated goose or a bunch of plug-in tulips. You will have to experiment with the positioning of decorative lighting as well as with various types of bulb before you get the effect you want.

1

2

CEILING AND WALL LIGHTS

1 *An antique brass and glass chandelier, now electrified. The ceiling rose from which it hangs has been disguised with a short length of coiled rope.*
2 *An ornate glass wall light. The cut glass beads reflect and deflect the candlelight.*

3

4

5

6

7

3 *A very delicate antique brass wall light, now electrified and used with small silk lampshades. The little bells that hang from the chains tinkle attractively in the slightest breeze.*
4 *Beautiful antique wall sconce for a single candle. The mirror reflector doubles its light output.*

5 *An interesting hanging lantern with a boule glass shade, part opaque and part cut glass in order to diffuse the light and cut out glare from beneath.*
6 *An antique brass and glass star lantern. These are now available as reproductions.*
7 *An exuberant terracotta wall sconce,*

now painted white and electrified, looks wonderful against the brightly painted wall. The little stiffened half-shades clip directly onto the light bulbs.

215

Flowers and Plants

Without any effort, and without much expense, flowers and plants will bring any room to life. They can automatically make a room feel lived in and will provide good focal points and fill up awkward gaps. When choosing fresh flowers pick something that enhances your colour scheme and do not forget that the container is as much a part of the arrangement as the contents. Go for more rather than less. An armful of autumn leaves in a simple jug has more impact than an orchid in a priceless vase.

Obviously real plants are much nicer than artificial ones, but if you are living in a flat with non-independent central heating and little in the way of light or ventilation then imitations may have to suffice. The best ones are made of silk and if placed realistically it will be hard to tell the difference.

Dried flowers are another alternative to fresh, which can prove expensive especially if purchased on a regular basis. You can make or commission an arrangement to match your colour scheme. I have often placed dried flower arrangements in empty fireplaces and used dried flower trees in corners where some height was required.

Plants look good in any room, so do not confine them to the obvious places. Some plants thrive in bathrooms, others will do well on shady landings. In kitchens, fresh herbs in terracotta planters will not only look attractive but enhance your cooking.

Inset *Little plant pots have been tucked into this terracotta bowl along with the cut flowers.*
1 A magnificent old-fashioned arrangement of old-fashioned garden

3

5

4

6

flowers takes its colour accent of pinky-purples, yellows and greens from the wall colour, the kilim table cover and the painting of anemones.

2 A simple arrangement in a simple, earthenware vase. A little of the garden has come indoors in the shape of a handful of cornflowers, lupins, cow

parsley and a single white rose.

3 & 4 Two arrangements using flowers of similar colours. One is tall and imposing and housed in a slender black and gold vase, the other is a sweet and charming bedside arrangement in a simple glass milk jug.

5 All the colours of the room are

collected together in this simple arrangement of garden flowers set into a brass cachepot.

6 A gleaming autumnal arrangement of evergreens and berries in a lovely hand-painted vase prove that an eye-catching and colourful arrangement can be achieved without a single bloom.

1

3

2

4

1 *Diverting attention from an unused black fireplace is a white jug full of white garden flowers and plenty of varied greenery.*
2 *A pair of matching arrangements, though simple in themselves, add dignity and proportion to the magnificent marble fireplace. The reds*

and greens have been deliberately chosen to tie in with the floral chintz fabric used for the curtains.
3 *A generous arrangement of roses, sweet peas and dark green leaves strike the correct chord in this rustic country setting.*
4 *A summertime treatment for a white-*

painted fireplace consists of a collection of jugs, a bunch of long-stemmed asters and two little pink posies.
5 *A light and airy conservatory that strikes just the right note between people and plants. The contrast of leaf shape, texture and colour makes a mass of house plants a year-long visual treat.*

USEFUL ADDRESSES

Most of the companies mentioned, apart from those listed below with their own London showrooms, supply goods only to the trade, which means that you have to go through a decorator to obtain them. In the UK, Spencer-Churchill Designs fabrics are available through over 500 outlets. Phone the Woodstock or London office for your nearest supplier, or for help with any aspect of interior design.

Spencer-Churchill Designs
55 Hollywood Road
London SW10 9HX
Tel: 071 376 5420
Fax: 071 376 3541

Woodstock Designs
7 High Street
Woodstock
Oxfordshire OX7 9XX
Tel: 0993 811887
Fax: 0993 813487

SUPPLIERS OF FABRICS AND WALLPAPERS WITH RETAIL SHOWROOMS

Colefax & Fowler
39 Brook Street
London W1Y 2JE
Tel: 071 493 2231

Cole & Son (Wallpapers) Ltd
18 Mortimer Street
London W1A 4BU
Tel: 071 580 2288

John Oliver Paints Ltd
33 Pembridge Road
London W 11 3HG
Tel: 071 221 6466

Designers Guild
277 King's Road
London SW3 5EN
Tel: 071 351 5775

Osborne & Little plc
304 King's Road
London SW3
Tel: 071 352 1456

SPENCER-CHURCHILL DESIGNS – EUROPEAN AND AUSTRALIAN DISTRIBUTORS

Nora Flinterman
Extend
Prins Van Wiedlaan 5
2242 CC Wassenaar
Netherlands

Monica Westerberg
Linnegatan 90
115 23 Stockholm
Sweden

Norsk System Design AS
Kongensgt 39
Boks 410
3201 Sandefjord
Norway

NO 7
Jaegersborg Alle
7 Dk 2920 Charlottenlund
Denmark

Tamise
8 Allée de Vandanges
BP 12 Marne La Valée
77313 Croissy Beaubourne
France

Hermitage Fabrics
Av 25 De Abril 13 B
2750 Cascais
Portugal

Ascraft Fabrics
57 Mallett Street,
Camperdown NSW 2050
Australia

US DISTRIBUTORS

Order fabrics through your decorator or contact the Spencer-Churchill Designs distributor in New York. The distributors listed below stock many of the other traditional, classic fabrics and trimmings mentioned in this book and, although they handle no retail business, they will be able to advise you. If you live in or near New York, visit the D&D Building where many distributors have their showrooms.

Cowton & Tout
D&D Building
10th Floor
979 3rd Avenue
NY, NY 10022
Tel: 212 753 4488

Clarence House
211 E. 58th Street
NY, NY 10022
Tel: 212 752 2890

SPENCER-CHURCHILL DESIGNS – US DISTRIBUTORS

Grey Watkins Ltd
D&D Building
979 3rd Avenue
NY, NY 10022
Tel: 212 371 2333

ACKNOWLEDGEMENTS

The author and the publishers would like to thank the following companies for their kind assistance. Some of the company names have been reduced to initials in the captions.

Afia Fabrics Limited, Anta, Busby & Busby, Bennison Fabrics, J. Brooke-Fairbairn & Co, G.P. & J. Baker, L & E Barnett (Trimmings) Ltd, Colefax & Fowler (C&F), Nina Campbell, Manuel Canovas, Cole & Son (Wallpapers) Ltd, Craigie Carpets, Coromandel, Dovedale Fabrics, Gainsborough Silk Weavers, Gallery of Antique Costume and Textiles, H.R.W. Antiques, Harris Fabrics, Hill & Knowles Limited, Jamasque, Jab International Furnishings Ltd, Marvic Textiles, Muraspec, Newgate Carpets, Nobilis Fontan, Henry Newbery, Osborne & Little plc, (O&L), H.A. Percheron Ltd, Pallu & Lake, Pierre Frey, Renwick and Clarke, Romo Fabrics (Nottm), Spencer-Churchill Designs Ltd (SCD), M. Short, Steeles Carpets, Arthur Sanderson & Sons Ltd, Stothert & Miles, Sussex Silks, Ian Sanderson, Textiles (FCD) Ltd, Dr Brian J Taylor, The Isle Mill Limited, Warners Fabrics, Caroline Ward Designs, Wemyss Houles, Zoffany Limited, Zimmer & Rhodes.

The author would like to thank the following for kindly allowing their homes to be photographed:
Mr & Mrs Colin Rosser, Mr & Mrs Roger Eckersley, The Hon. Robin & Mrs Cayzer, Lord Rayleigh, Mr & Mrs Roderick Peacock, Mr & Mrs Ian Bond, The Hon. Peter & Mrs Ward, Mr John Quitter, Miss Sarah St. George, Mrs Eric Towler, The Rt. Hon. Baron Waterpark.

PICTURE CREDITS

All photographs have been taken specially for this book by Andreas von Einsiedel except for the following:
Courtesy of the Duke & Duchess of Marlborough, photo Jeremy Whitaker: right p67, p69, p71, p78. Garden Picture Library: both p49. Derry Moore: 1 p160, 4 p163, 1 p172, 1 p176, 2 p176, 4 p177, 5 p177, 5 p187, 2 p190, Inset p196, 1 p202, 2 p202, 4 p209. National Portrait Gallery, London: above p67. Elizabeth Whiting & Associates: Andreas von Einsiedel 6 p155, 3 p159, 4 p181, 3 p185, Inset p188, 6 p189, 3 p190, 4 p191, 3 p193, 4 p193, 1 p196, 3 p197, 1 p200, 2 p200, 4 p201, 5 p201, 6 p201, 4 p203, 5 p207, 5 p209, 2 p210, 4 p211, 5 p211, 3 p213, 5 p217; Michael Crockett 4 p161, 5 p197; Michael Dunne 4 p206; Di Lewis 1 p218; Tom Leighton 3 p210, 4 p218; Spike Powell 1 p198; Jerry Tubby 1 p210; Peter Woloszynski 1 p208, 6 p209. Andy Williams Photo Library: p46, p47, p48, p50; Neil Bradford, Leila Corbett Designs, John Fowler, Nicholas Haslam, Erik Karson, Carole King, Anthony Little, Barbara Palmer.

INDEX

Numbers in italics to refer to illustrations.